FAUST: *A Tragedy, Part 1*

JOHANN WOLFGANG von GOETHE

FAUST

A Tragedy, PART ONE

TRANSLATED BY ALICE RAPHAEL

INTRODUCTION AND NOTES BY JACQUES BARZUN

———————

HOLT, RINEHART AND WINSTON, INC.

**NEW YORK • CHICAGO • SAN FRANCISCO • ATLANTA • DALLAS
MONTREAL • TORONTO • LONDON • SYDNEY**

Translation copyright, 1930, by Alice Raphael
Translation copyright ©, 1955, by Alice Raphael
Introduction and Notes copyright ©, 1955,
by Jacques Barzun
Printed in the United States of America
All Rights Reserved
Typography by Stefan Salter
Library of Congress Catalog Card Number: 55-8417

SBN: 03-007815-6
01234   68   191817161514131211

Introduction

Goethe's *Faust* was *the* book of the Romantic period. In an age which produced many great novelties—the heroic verse tales of Byron, the vivid historical novels of Scott, the ironic psychological studies of Stendhal, the vast realistic panorama of Balzac—Goethe's drama kept its position of pre-eminence, and for one sufficient reason: it stood forth as the complete presentment of modern man's doubts and aspirations.

The twentieth century, for equally good reasons, finds the work less satisfying, on which account it forgets to read it and speaks of it at third or fourth hand. But ignorance and partial neglect do not lessen its importance, any more than they dim the pleasure and enlightenment to be drawn from it. Indeed, one *has* to read the poem if one is to grasp the meaning and feel the force of not a few utterances of yesterday and today. What, for instance, does Spengler mean in *The Decline of the West* when he calls our epoch Faustian? What is Carlyle (echoed by Matthew Arnold) saying when he counsels, "Close thy Byron; open thy Goethe"? Why does Santayana, writing shortly before his death to criticize the American spirit, complain that "we are still in the laboratory of Dr. Faust"? And why does Thomas Mann, in his novels and essays, so persistently return to the subject of Goethe's life and, without awakening a like reminiscence in the reader, remind himself of the great poet?

Again, even though one may care nothing about Gounod's opera on the theme of Faust, nor about Liszt's symphonic poem, Wagner's overture, or Berlioz's music drama, it is clear from these and much else in our musical repertoire that the Faust legend as Goethe bequeathed it to the nineteenth century is an integral part of our culture. Painters, too, have been inspired by it, no less than musicians, historians, and poets. We think with it and talk to one another in its terms: Mephisto, Gretchen, Auerbach's tavern, the witches on the Brocken are but a few of the symbols that were given life and currency by Goethe's unexampled, mysterious, and powerful creation. It stands there at the threshold of our formative days, a challenge to our understanding. When we know the work we may hope to know ourselves better—besides knowing better our oppressive fathers of the previous century.

Perhaps the quickest way to penetrate the meaning of *Faust* is to reflect on the ambiguity of the word "modern." In one of its senses the term is used to describe the mind and deeds of Western man since about 1500. In another equally common usage it applies to any idea or person characteristic of the latest age, the 170 years since the French Revolution of 1789.

In the first sense, the things we associate with modern man include the Renaissance, Protestantism, the humanists' passion for the art of Greece and Rome, the forward strides of physical science, the political forms of mercantilism and monarchy. We personify all these: Copernicus, Bacon, Shakespeare, Galileo, Luther, Newton, Louis XIV.

With the word "modern" in the second sense we are apt to associate first the great anonymous movements and ideas which, being still potent, cause us anguish and evoke our doubt or distrust: the Enlightenment, Liberty–Equality–Fraternity, the Industrial Revolution, Utilitarianism, the nation-state, philosophic naturalism and scientism, which is to say the belief in man's evolving powers and the decline of religious faith.

In short, viewed from one standpoint the man of the twentieth century deems himself the lucky heir of half a millennium of expanding thought which has changed the face of the globe as well as his conception of himself; and from another point of view, which sees in the foreground total war and perpetual revolution, modern man feels himself orphaned, uprooted, outcast, disinherited—and he finds the cause of his misery in the very same expanding thoughts that have changed the face of the globe as well as his conception of himself.

Whatever opinion one may hold concerning the rights, the wrongs, and the remedies of this situation, it remains true that the two moments of great change within the half millennium were the Protestant Reformation in the sixteenth century and the combined political, industrial, and psychological revolution in the late eighteenth and early nineteenth. To this second moment we give the name of Romanticism, and we record our sense of its nearness and significance by speaking of the earlier time as "the old regime." The old regime is already far enough away for us to idealize it. We forget its violence and oppression because we long for its real or apparent stability—the stability which it lost between 1750 and 1850 when we were catapulted into the *modern* modern world, for whose disturbances we blame the revolutionary Romantic spirit.

Now, the relevance of these general truths to *Faust* is that its author composed it during the passage of Western civilization from its relatively static condition to its present one of acceleration. Goethe was born in 1749 and lived until 1832. During sixty years of this life span, in round numbers from 1770 to 1830, he worked at, or dreamed on, or shied away from the subject *Faust*. Unlike any other great work, this one, which is peculiarly permeated by the feeling of time, grew with its own times. More than that, it grew out of the legend of another time, which happened to be that of the earlier epoch of change, the time of Renaissance and Reformation. In all ways, therefore, the likelihood was great that such a work, developing with the mind of a thinking poet, would be what the nineteenth century in fact took it to be—an epitome of the modern age.

Yet at first blush it is difficult to see how the story of a middle-aged intellectual and dabbler in the occult who makes a compact with the Devil, consorts with witches, and brings an innocent girl to ruin, can reflect or embody the grave issues of a civilization's passage from kingship to democracy, authority to individualism, handicraft to industry, Christian dogma to agnostic science. The very plot of the play seems hopelessly old-fashioned, and when the book itself is read, it is found to contain no direct reference to any of these issues. Rather, it presents a haphazard succession of scenes, mostly in doggerel, interlarded with broad jokes, ribald songs, and occasionally a passage of lyrical nature poetry or philosophizing about God and the universe. Even as drama the work fails to meet expectations. The action is fitful, the dialogue argumentative rather than passionate, and the most spectacular moments—such as the witches' revel— are clearly unrealizable on the stage.

To these handicaps must be added the ambiguity inseparable from any mention of *Faust:* does the speaker mean Part I, which everybody knows at least by hearsay, or does he mean both parts, the second of which only scholars and critics are supposed to have studied? Part II has the reputation of being obscure and important, but it is clear enough that a sequel is not absolutely required by the self-contained first play—except in so far as the very end of the second shows how Faust is "saved." We knew from that outset that he was going to be, but the mode of his salvation affects our interpretation of everything that happens in Part I. What the candid reader faces, then, is the paradox of a great dramatic work which is rarely played and seldom read entire, which is obscure or ambiguous in all but its traditional plot, and which nevertheless is felt to illuminate matters it does not visibly treat of.

A sufficient rejoinder to this criticism might be that many other masterpieces are likewise incompletely read and require imagination to appreciate their form and penetrate their mystery. Hamlet (which we seldom see entire) is a veritable graveyard for solutions to the riddle it presents, and Dante's *Divine Comedy* (of which the last part is also the preserve of scholars) calls for even more reading-in than *Faust*, despite its still simpler plot.

And the historical fact remains that the Romanticist generations between 1830 and 1870 were not deterred by paradox or difficulty. They read *Faust*—like an open book, saying, "This is a faithful image of ourselves." In other words, through its old plot and medieval machinery *Faust* depicts man and his destiny in a manner exactly matching the idea that Western humanity had of itself a century ago.

The core of that idea is restated by Goethe in a passage relating, it so happens, to Shakespeare:

The highest achievement possible to a man is the full consciousness of his own feelings and thoughts, for this gives him the means of knowing intimately the heart of others.

Every word of this maxim could be the subject of an extended commentary. It would be filled with such terms and phrases as Individualism, Experience, and the Eternal Feminine; "two souls within one breast," "the garment of the Deity," and "the night-side of Nature"; the infinite thirst for knowledge, the superiority of striving over achieving, and the primacy of the Act over the Word. Most of these come from the text of *Faust* and have established themselves in the language as names for new principles or realities that Goethe found or expressed in his effort to reach "the full consciousness of his own feelings and thoughts." And together with their context these formulas compose the image of man which Romanticism recognized as its own.

But we must not think of *Faust* as having been designed from the beginning to fulfill this external and abstract purpose. The abstraction reflects only a judgment passed on the work after it was done. Goethe was the poet of Experience in more ways than one; and, as he himself said, he never wrote a line except about events and feelings he had himself undergone, these including of course his imaginings of the unknown.

The first notion of *Faust* came to him from quite a simple feeling, with which young men everywhere are likely to sympathize: he was bored with his studies. Not yet twenty years old, he was by his father's wish studying law at the University of Leipzig and, finding his textbooks dreary, was attracted by magic and the occult. A year later, having transferred to the University of Strasbourg, the idea of a poem on Dr. Faust took more definite shape. But, like all young men of talent and passion, he still suffered from moods; by turns exuberant and depressed, he felt hemmed in, and his cloistered energies bred boredom, melancholy, and thoughts of suicide—precisely as in *Faust*.

We know that Goethe was taking note of these storms and stresses of his inner life because five years later, in 1775, he gave them artistic form in the little novel which made his reputation: *The Sorrows of Young Werther*. Werther commits suicide, not solely because of frustrated love, but also because he is balked in his ambitions: the world, he feels, denies him everything, and his will destroys his life. When Faust is on the verge of suicide, his plight is somewhat different: it is not that the world denies him his wish but that it has nothing to give him. Instead of destroying himself he sets out on a voyage for the rediscovery of reality behind the visible world. He lives by making a career out of his dissatisfaction. He has the Devil's help, to be sure, but it is his own distress that propels him. As the Italian scholar Borgese has finely observed, "It is his inability to sit that destines him to soar." And this is the reason why Faust is not merely a character in a play, or even a type commonly found, but a collective or universal hero.

His likeness to the men of the Romantic period consists in the fact that they too, coming after the French
Revolution and Napoleon, found themselves in a world that
had nothing to give them. It was seemingly well ordered;
life followed ancient conventions and aimed at stability
according to bourgeois standards. But the young, the articu-
late, the idealists were bored by an aim that called for
prudence rather than energy. They were revolted by a
conventional order that encouraged conformity rather than
discovery. Those that did not commit suicide like Werther
pledged themselves to rediscover nothing less than the entire
universe, the inner world of man and the outer world of
nature: they became Faustian by the decree of time and
temperament.

The Faust of Goethe's schoolboy feelings did not, of
course, achieve this representative stature at one bound. To
understand his final complexity, which is his modernity, one
must see how he developed under Goethe's hand from the
rather crude Renaissance figure perserved by tradition.

There lived in Germany in the early 1500's an actual
John Faust, a charlatan leading a vagrant life but in touch
with learned men as well as with leaders of the Reformation.
Because he performed feats of magic, or boasted of doing so,
he was said to have sold his soul to the Devil. He came, in
fact, to a mysterious and violent end about the year 1540.
The fascinated horror with which stories of his exploits
were repeated, mixed with the eternal popular distrust of
intellect and science, kept his memory alive until, in 1587, a
printed account of his life was published.

Ever since the story of Eve and the serpent, mortals
have made compacts with the Devil to obtain knowledge
and power, and the retelling of the event has always aroused
strong emotions of envy and fear. In the first sixteenth-
century Faust tale, however, we are shocked to discover
what that age of faith most desired—and doubtless needed:

it was food. The passion that dominates Faust is not for power, knowledge, or the sensual delights of love; he longs chiefly to eat his fill. He also wants clothing and pocket money, and by way of entertainment he would like to "fly among the stars." We need not dwell on the up-to-dateness of this pastime, but we should remember to the end of our reading of Goethe the original Faust's first wish. Later in his adventures the primitive Faust is eager to marry, but his helpful demon Mephisto shows him that he needn't trouble about a legal union. Finally, Mephisto has him read a book on human destiny and the origin of the world, which re-awakens Faust's learning and makes him foresee his awful end.

This edifying tale was shortly translated into English and captured the imagination of the young poet Marlowe, who made of it his tragedy *Dr. Faustus*. In it the hero is ennobled by desiring chiefly power and experience. He is punished in the orthodox manner, but the spectator feels that the poet sides with Faustus in his rebellion against dogma, custom, and the trammels of mortal flesh.

At this point one might have thought that Faust was in a fair way to become an important symbol. A great poet had lifted the figure of the trickster and magician to a plane where his deeds amounted to a criticism of life. The time seemed ripe; for the sixteenth century was an early Romanticism in its passion for discovery and introspection: its buccaneers explored the New World, and its art and philosophy repudiated the "old regime," which then meant the feudal order and the medieval faith. Man seemed once more a creature of infinite possibilities, the maker of his own fate on earth, which was the true theater of his actions. Marlowe gives us a hint of this new humanism and secularism when he has Mephisto reply to Faustus's question on earth:

Why, this is hell, nor am I out of it.

Yet only ten years later the philosopher Giordano Bruno, whom Goethe was later to read, was burned at the stake for bidding "heroic enthusiasts" grasp the idea of an impersonal God everywhere alive in the visible world. The Reformation had indeed given the loose to speculation, but orthodoxy was strong, and the English Faust, still a heretic, did not enlarge into a model of the New Man.

Far from taking on richer meaning, the legendary figure soon fell below his original state. Strolling players brought him back to Germany, where he became the butt of slapstick. After a while he survived only as a stock character in puppet shows. It was in this guise that Goethe as a child first heard of him. But the times were obviously conspiring to resurrect him, for in 1759, when Goethe was ten years old, the German poet and critic Lessing sketched a serious Faust play and wrote the opening scene. Lessing was then beginning his crusade against the artificial French tragedies which the cultural imperialism of France had long enforced upon German taste. It was logical that he should choose a native subject, popular rather than courtly, yet capable of elevated meaning, while at the same time he preached the free naturalistic technique of Shakespeare.

Matters stood thus when Goethe's mind turned to the old story and its hero in 1769 or '70. The further transformations of the character followed the several stages through which Goethe's vast work moved toward completion. These changes are intimately connected with his life, and it would take a book to retrace them. Only a few decisive steps and dates can be noted here. One date is 1790, when in response to his friends' demand, Goethe published large portions of the poem they knew in manuscript. Clearly labeled "A fragment," this series of scenes is the core of what we know as Part I. In 1808 the completed first play appeared, and in 1832—posthumously, though it had been finished the year before—Part II.

As for the decisive steps in Goethe's conception of Faust, they are at least four, and all have to do with Time.

The first is implied in the conversation between God and Devil in Heaven, imitated from a similar dialogue in the Book of Job. Before the play begins, Goethe makes it clear that Faust will not be damned. This alters not only the plot of the legend but also the meaning of tragedy, by shifting its place from the hereafter to the here and now. It isn't because Faust, after much travail, may endure eternal torment that he is a tragic figure; it is because he is on earth and a thinking being. The drama begins in torment, which continues unbroken until Faust has traversed the small world of private life, depicted in Part I, and the big world of the Emperor's Court, or public life, depicted in Part II. And the torment comes from the awareness that man is at once wretched and great. He is wretched because he is a limited, mortal creature; he is great because his mind embraces the whole universe and knows its own wretchedness.

No ordinary satisfaction can quench Faust's desires; forever he sees and wants something beyond. The ultimate bliss would be to feel at one with nature, through knowledge not merely intellectual but emotional also, virtually instinctive; whereas all learning serves but to make Faust more self-conscious and isolated, till he scarcely feels that he lives. Clearly, this defines the situation of modern civilized man, whose increasing knowledge makes him more and more self-critical, anxious, beset by doubts, and hence more and more an alien in the natural world that is his only home.

For this reason—and this is the second great change in the conception of Faust—the terms of the bargain with Mephisto are entirely new. It is no longer the old deal by which a soul is exchanged for bodily pleasures. Faust undertakes to serve the Devil only if one of the attractions that the Devil spreads before him makes Faust say to the passing moment,

> If ever to the moment I should say,
> "Oh, stay! Thou art so fair!"

In other words, magic for Faust, science for modern man, enlarges his sphere of action. Each is committed to trying everything. Mephisto (and science) keep on producing opportunities addressed to the senses, for man does not shed his body merely by becoming interested in the quest for ultimate truth. But the result of trial and error is for both a round of desire, disillusion, disgust, and despair.

Across this headlong flight from misery comes, in Goethe's play, the figure of Gretchen.* The story of her love for Faust, her undoing, her misdeeds, her death and that of her brother, are in themselves touching and true. As is shown by Gounod's opera and the public's notion of the whole subject, these scenes constitute the heart of the Faust matter. But the love story is also symbolic. It affirms, among other things, the reality of time. What has happened to the unfortunate Gretchen cannot be erased, undone. There is no realm where her sorrows are "made good" or her acts wiped out by punishment. To be sure, the supernatural machinery of the play is used by the poet to assure us that her faults are those of an innocent, "bedeviled" person, not those of a hardened and scheming criminal: she is "saved." But the wonderful realism of her depiction is there to remind us that she, her brother, and their mother—all killed, like her newborn child, as a result of her love—are persons to be thought of as ends in themselves and not as instruments of God playing parts in a moral tale.

It is this irreducible fact that causes Faust's first unselfish

---

* Gretchen is one of the diminutives of the heroine's name, Margarete, which means pearl.

pang. The existence of other people is brought home to him with a sudden violence which punctures his lofty mood and makes his high speculations shrink to triviality. To a feeling being, what can the flights of art, philosophy, and religion weigh against the present, actual pain of another human being? Critics who find a discrepancy of scale between the opening of *Faust I* and its close, because philosophic doubt is "important" and a betrayed girl is "unimportant," are criticizing in the air, thinking abstractly, and missing Goethe's point about the primacy of the concrete. The premise which he makes universal by affirming that "In the beginning was the Act" (not "the Word," as in the gospel) finds a humble but proper illustration in the trivial but truly horrifying details of Gretchen in prison—the locked door, the wanderings of her poor simple mind, the resistless march of time. On earth she is doomed, and her blood is upon Faust's head.

His instant horror when he is reminded by the news of her plight that society does exist and that it is not merely a backdrop for his introspective journey depends upon the third significant change that Goethe introduced into the traditional story. Usually Faust was represented as an old necromancer, thus accounting for his mastery of diabolical secrets. And at first the young Goethe changed him to a young man full of his own melancholy and passion. But as the poet matured, his hero matured with him, and we now find Faust in his study to be a man of middle age—the dangerous age when professional experience and success breed the conviction that the world is stale and all past efforts vain. To lead him astray, Mephisto makes Faust young again, and he loves like an ardent youth. Yet he remembers his worldly wisdom, as we can see in the prompt disgust he feels in Auerbach's tavern, and still more meaningfully in the final scenes of his dismay at what he has done.

Unlike most heroes, he has in fact two lives, and by their juxtaposition he learns what is missing from each. In

the first, before the play, too much conventional occupation
and withdrawal into bookish lore have withered his heart.
He feels cut off from both the grand and the dark forces of
nature and finds life worthless. In the second, appetite and a
desperate courage bring him closer to the heart of nature
and carry him through the heights and depths of feeling,
but he forgets until too late that he is not alone in the universe. If he were a youth on his first pilgrimage, like the
heroes of many a "novel of education," he could find ex-
cuses, either in himself or in the eyes of others. But his being
a man with an intellectual and moral past doubles his guilt,
and he suffers a new form of anguish far worse than doubt
and emptiness of soul, for it involves more than himself. His
powerlessness is now no longer a defect but a punishment.

The one thing he has gained, or regained, is an erotic
outlook upon the world, and it is this, presumably, which
propels him through the adventures of Part II. By "erotic"
here we mean a disposition to love, accept, feel *with*—in
contrast to the attitude that rejects, denies, scorns, and hates.
Eroticism in this generalized sense is perhaps the one element which Romantic with a large R and romantic with a
small one have in common. The historical Romanticists
sometimes seem silly to us because they were disposed to
admire, love, worship. But this willingness to love also denotes courage, venturesomeness, the facing of risks. It is
obviously possible never to be fooled and never to appear
foolish—always play safe. It takes a self-confidence which
we of the twentieth century have evidently lost to face not
only disappointment and ridicule but also suffering and
irreparable loss.

In his second play, Goethe seems to trace the erotic
principle to its source in the weird scene of Faust's visit to
"The Mothers," but the less mysterious aspects of love he
enshrines in the closing maxim that "the Eternal Feminine
draws us onward," as well as in the fulfillment of Faust's
destiny and his death.

The Eternal Feminine means a good deal more than the proverb which says that love makes the world go round, or even than the definition "God is love." The Eternal Feminine is nothing less than the symbol of life, the irrational ground and irresistible force which is prior to all else, reason included. And Goethe's phrase does but sum up what is shown throughout the entire poem, that nature is alive—an organism, not a machine; that all things are linked with one another by a genetic bond (that is, productive and re-productive), as against the formal or generic bond that we perceive when we merely classify and fail to see life unfolding in Time. Goethe, we must remember, was an early evolutionist whose *Metamorphosis of Plants* revolutionized botany, and whose philosophy and poetry alike repudiated the materialistic mechanism current in the eighteenth century.

His awareness of life-in-time brings us to the fourth and last great twist he gave to the Faust story, the momentous resolution found at the very end of Part II and indispensable for a true reading of Part I. Having traversed the "big world" and its follies, Faust finds himself, at an advanced age, employed in reclaiming land from the sea, that it may be cultivated. He feels death upon him, and though he wants to complete the work to which he is committed heart and soul, he cannot. The vision of it must suffice and it suggests to him that if realized he could say to the passing minute, "Oh, stay! Thou art so fair!" He dies. "Time is lord," as Mephisto says, thinking he has at last won Faust. But the Heavenly Host intervene, and the Devil is cheated of his prey.

The moral is clear, and possibly surprising, for Faust has described a complete circle: he started as a physician ministering to the well-being of his fellow men; he ends as a civil engineer accomplishing another part of the same task. More than that, we seem for one dizzy moment to have spiraled back to the original Faust, who used his magic to bring him food. The parallel is not exact, but it does remind us that mankind's first necessity is to eat and survive. Whoever contributes to that result obviously loves humanity, loves life. What Goethe would have us believe is that happiness, even for a lofty spirit, consists in devotion to an enterprise of this kind. That this conclusion was no special or transitory one is shown by the fact that in the last part of his "novel of education," *Wilhelm Meister*, Goethe has his hero embark as a surgeon to a group of emigrants to America.

The later Goethe was clearly imbued with the "American spirit" in so far as this implies working at material tasks for the general welfare. Our century's objections to *Faust* on a doctrinal basis are therefore a little hard to countenance, for they bear down equally on the boundless desires and reckless self-seeking of the beginning Faust and on the selfless disciplined manager of public works whom we find at the end. If, as W. H. Auden has ably argued, our age wants poems that symbolize the building of cities rather than the exploring of deserts, one would suppose that Faust was the ideal hero—the hero as city-planner. But Faust doubtless felt unsought-for bliss in his collective task because he had first gone through his wilderness alone. We today resent both phases because we have lost his erotic attitude. An unpurged, sneaking, low-grade romanticism in ourselves makes the early Faust appear to us heroic but foolish, while the later Faust seems shrunken and crass.

The question is not, of course, whether we should take Faust as a model, like the men of previous generations, but whether he is *a* model deserving imaginative credence. The historian of today may be forced to conclude that the poem and our reality are still too close together. Our ears are too full of the dying echoes of Romanticism to heed the original voice. To Carlyle's advice about closing Byron (revolt, exploration) and opening Goethe (the gospel of work), we feel like shouting: "Close them both!" We are not even in a mood to wonder why a scornful, lacerated spirit like Swift should set down as indisputable truth the importance of making two blades of grass grow where only one grew before. We make them grow, mechanically, without loving mankind, because we have largely ceased to love ourselves, and such remnants of the power of Eros as we possess grope to find their object in the deities of orthodox religion.

A cycle is thereby closed, for it was those deities' displacement or redefinition which marked the course of Faust's career, from his magic tricks in Luther's day, through Marlowe's and Lessing's and Goethe's reincarnations of his will to truth.

In comparing our own doubts about man's destiny with those Goethe pictured and resolved for his century, we must remember that a poem persuades by its art, not its arguments. And here too, with respect to art, some find it an effort to experience anew in our day the electrifying force which *Faust* (the first part alone sufficing) exerted on its contemporaries. Not that anyone who reads German could even now remain insensible to Goethe's poetical power. *Faust* contains many perfect utterances, high moments of lyric and satiric art. It is the work as a constructed whole that has to be justified to an age not merely critical but expert at carping.

For the demands that any period makes upon art vary in relation to the possibilities and satisfactions that life itself holds out, and if today we are extremely hard to please it is because our mastery over nature is almost complete yet does not bring us the expected sensations. We are virtually omnipotent in the realm of Faust the engineer, but this only underscores the imperfection we feel within. We complain of frustration, anxiety, and guilt. Accordingly we require art to show with scorn, or with a promise of harmony hereafter, the paradox of power and impotence peculiar to ourselves. We ask for tough mindlessness or moral symmetry, for Hemingway or Dante.

As we know, the questing Faust was balked by different circumstances; his anxiety and guilt came at the close of his first exploration and were purged by the end of his pilgrimage. Hence to recount his journey Goethe could properly use the "open" and varied form, part lyrical, part dramatic, which Shakespeare had exemplified and Lessing advocated. Marlowe also considered it suitable to the subject, since he cast his drama in fourteen scenes whose continuity is supplied by the spectator's imagination. The twenty-five scenes of Goethe's *Faust I* constitute a still more "ideal" action. Even though their presentation on the stage has again and again proved effective, the drama takes place in the mind's eye, a screenless motion picture. Seen in that way, all the work's diversities but one are firmly held together. That one exception is Scene XXII, the "Walpurgis Night's Dream," which is a series of mediocre epigrams on forgotten subjects. Goethe was ill-advised to insert them in place of the climax he had aptly conceived to end the diabolic sequence—a piece of unprintable naturalism, of which some discarded surviving sheets give us an idea.

Apart from this lapse, the validity of the thesis which the Poet, the Manager, and the Comic Person set forth in their prefatory wrangle is unimpaired: a play—a modern play—is a compromise among the conflicting demands for plot, fun, and rhyme; or, again, a true representation of the world must fuse thought, passion, and humor. In search of these we travel from Faust's study to Auerbach's tavern, from the Witches' Kitchen to the garden where Faust courts Gretchen. Everything falls into place and serves the recognized purposes of the playwright: characterizing

complex and changeable human beings; creating by manifold detail the illusion of a complete world, and thickening
the action with philosophic contrasts or worldly ironies.
Thus the dialogues with Wagner confront professional
learning with inspired truth-seeking; the Garden scene in
its double pairing yields the contrast between conventional
marriage and passionate love; and by their incessant bicker-
ing Faust and Mephisto mutually debunk each other. A
perpetual irony plays upon every position, the cynical no
less than the heroic. This in itself is drama, and the joining
of the two tempers is a psychological disclosure of self-
conscious modern man—Goethe to begin with, and any of
us who look into his magic mirror.

What holds together these "two souls within one
breast" is the force typified by the witches and embodied
in superstition—demonic energy or the push of life. If this
notion seems to contradict the labeling of Mephisto as
"the spirit that ever denies," we have only to recall Blake's
assertion that Energy, miscalled Evil, is the core of Reason
as well as the only life; a proposition which Freud ampli-
fied when he found coexisting in each of us with the lust
for life some dark impulse he called the death wish. But
the words in each case play the perception false. Ever since
Rousseau, whose influence on Goethe's art was great, introspective minds have known that life is an element that
defies analysis, while at the same time it seems compounded
of opposites. It cannot, therefore, be talked about in geometrical propositions but only in poetic ones—parable,
allegory, myth. The tone must match the mystery and
force of the phenomenon—no longer the composed and
witty utterances of a Voltaire, but the divining riddles of
the poets. Pope's *Essay on Man* must yield to the less lucid
but all-encompassing art of Shakespeare.

It was the pulse of this conviction which, running all
through *Faust*, stirred the Romanticists to admiration. The

work would have failed of its effect had the doctrine been couched in the rhetoric of neoclassic art. The new grandeur must on the contrary spring from extreme contrasts— Mephisto's mocking doggerel and Faust's apostrophe to the Sublime Spirit; Gretchen's sweetness and the obscenities of the witches' sabbath; the intellectual doubts of Faust and the small-town gossip that moves Marthe, Valentin, and Gretchen's companions. It may indeed be said that the great artistic innovation in *Faust* is its willing vulgarity. For the first time since Shakespeare, a work of high intention took account of the low and small and commonplace.

This is not to exclude the comic writers, and particularly Molière, from the class of poets of high intentions who create with trivia. But the distinction must be kept between a work whose scene is the universe and any other whose scene is society. Molière, like his contemporary, Pascal, doubtless felt immortal longings of a pre-Faustian sort, but he quelled them even as he expressed them in *The Misanthrope*. Molière sides with the resigned and reasonable man who acknowledges the supremacy of society by conforming to it. Faust's role is to be unreasonable for the best of reasons— those to which Shaw gave general form in one of his "Maxims for Revolutionists":

The reasonable man adapts himself to the world: the unreasonable one persists in trying to adapt the world to himself. Therefore all progress depends on the unreasonable man.

Without arguing the question, What is Progress? one may say that by taking cognizance of unreason in this special sense, the unreason of change, movement, becoming (or as today's jargon calls it: the dynamic and dialectical), *Faust* is justified not only on historical but on artistic grounds. The changeful and restless are bound to discard symmetrical form and to call for the artfully irregular. Gothic construction replaces the solemn front of geometrical reason, flouts propriety by accepting the vulgar, and swings through the whole range of incompatible yet undeniable emotions. *Faust* is a tragedy, yet there is genuine laughter in it. Does anyone laugh in *The Divine Comedy?*

The question need not arise except in a comparison of styles such as preoccupied Goethe during all his mature years. He had lived as a youth through the rebellious time which in German literature bears the name of Storm and Stress; he had then produced works like *Werther* and *Götz von Berlichingen*, which answered to the description "Romantic" in the narrow sense. Nonetheless his admiration for the classic style as the eighteenth century saw it remained great. He naturally desired like other men the contentment of a mind at peace, and his love of order, of recognized beauty, was steadily re-enforced by his studies, his long stay in Italy, and his practice of academic painting. For years on end he laid *Faust* aside to work upon poems regularly constructed and expressive of serenity. In addition, his work at Weimar as court official and theater director strengthened from day to day his love of social order.

But this same business responsibility, together with his scientific and religious meditations, also proved from day to day that life, high or low, cannot be permanently set and fixed. The eternal and immovable can be conceived, but it cannot be found. The conception of it may even modify the shapes of life but cannot refashion it into a different thing having the perfection of stillness. How to reconcile the ideal vision and the no less visible fact became Goethe's chief task as man and artist. He kept coming back to the contradiction and its parts. For example, the temptation of the master spirit to coerce and control is given touching expression in an episode near the end of *Faust II*, in which the hero, impatient to extend his sphere of benevolent action, orders the destruction of the cottage where the aged Philemon and Baucis are ending their days. The welfare planner, so to say, begins his good works by a crime. Again in the second *Faust*, Goethe composed a "Classic-Romantic Walpurgisnight" in which the styles contending for his imagination were to be held in equipoise. Helen of Troy, typifying classical beauty, weds the romanticist Faust and gives birth to the harmonious modern, Euphorion.

To this parable Goethe recurs in prose when discussing Shakespeare, and we infer from his words how deliberate and just his aesthetic choices were when he adapted the forms of his Renaissance model to his own needs. We can measure also the degree to which he was, even late in life, a conscious Romanticist:

> Instead of singing the praises of our Romanticism so exclusively and sticking to it so uncritically—our Romanticism which need not be chidden or rejected—and thus obscuring its strong, solid, practical aspect, we should rather attempt to make this great fusion between the old and the new, even though it does seem inconsistent and paradoxical. All the more should we make the attempt, because a great and unique master [Shakespeare], to whom we give homage above all others, has already most effectively accomplished this miracle.

How far the miracle was repeated in *Faust* will ever remain a question for each reader and judge. But no judgment will bear on the stylistic issue, that is, on the art of *Faust*, if it neglects the principle which made it what it is and which Goethe originally drew from his mode of apprehending life. Once again and for the last time, Faust, speaking for Goethe, tells us how to reconcile, in art or in life, the order that means freedom and the passion that denotes life:

> Yes, of this truth I am convinced—
> This is wisdom's ultimate word:
> Only he deserves this life in freedom
> Who daily earns it all anew.

JACQUES BARZUN

CHRONOLOGY OF GOETHE'S LIFE

1749	August 28, Goethe born in Frankfort-on-the-Main
1765–1768	Goethe at the University of Leipzig; also studies painting with Adam Friedrich Oeser
1770–1771	Goethe at Strasbourg to resume legal studies
1773	*Götz von Berlichingen*, an historical drama
1774	*The Sorrows of Young Werther*, a psychological novel
1774–1775	First parts of *Faust I* written
1775	Goethe goes to Weimar where, with a few absences, he spent the rest of his life
1778	*Wilhelm Meister*, Book I
1784	Goethe discovers the intermaxillary bone in man (previously thought an exclusively animal feature)
1786–1788	Journey to Italy; *Faust* recast
1788	*Egmont*, a psychological drama
1790	*Faust: A Fragment; The Metamorphosis of Plants*
1791–1817	Goethe serves as stage manager of Weimar theater
1794–1805	Goethe-Schiller correspondence
1798	*Hermann and Dorothea*, a love story of the French Revolution
1801	*Faust I* finished
1808	*Faust: A Tragedy (Part I)* published; Interview with Napoleon during Congress of Erfurt
1809	*The Elective Affinities*, a novel
1811–1832	*Poetry and Truth*, an autobiography
1819	*The Metamorphosis of Animals*
1821–1829	*Wilhelm Meister's Pilgrimage*

Bibliographical Note

After a first reading in one's own language, a foreign classic should be read again, preferably in the original or, if this is beyond one's powers, in another translation. *Faust I* has been translated more than fifty times into English; at least twenty translations became well known between 1823 and the end of the nineteenth century. Of these, three are suggested for further reading: J. Anster (1835), reissued in the World's Classics together with Marlowe's *Dr. Faustus* and an introduction by A. W. Ward; Anna Swanwick (1849) in Bohn's Classics, with a useful bibliography; and Bayard Taylor (1870) in the Modern Library. The foregoing are all in verse. An inexpensive modern rendering in prose is that by Bayard Quincy Morgan (Liberal Arts Press, New York, 1954). The German text of Part I is available, with an excellent introduction and notes, in the edition by Calvin Thomas (D. C. Heath & Company, Boston, 1892 and ff.), or in the same publisher's edition by Heffner, Rehder, and Twaddell (1954).

For a survey of the life and character of Goethe, the best book to begin with is still George Henry Lewes's *Life of Goethe* (1855), now in the Everyman Library. The latest by an English scholar is Barker Fairley's *A Study of Goethe* (1947). Between these in point of time, and valuable for its special temper, is J. G. Robertson's *Goethe* (1927).

When the reader is familiar with the outline of Goethe's career, he may take up the autobiography *Poetry and Truth from My Own Life,* either in J. Oxenford's translation (Bohn Library, n.d.) or in R. O. Moon's (Public Affairs Press, New York, 1949). The entertaining *Conversations with Eckermann* (and Soret) are found in John Oxenford's translation (1850), republished in the Bohn and Everyman series.

As the bicentenary year 1949 approached, a quantity of Goethe anthologies and volumes of criticism began to appear. The fullest of these is *Goethe: The Story of a Man*, edited by Ludwig Lewisohn (2 vols.; New York, 1949). The contents are wholly in Goethe's own words or those of his contemporaries, and they form an excellent narrative for the reader who knows some political and cultural history. This background is obtainable in part from *Goethe's World as Seen in Letters and Memoirs*, edited by Berthold Biermann (New York, 1949), which contains sketches by and of such people as Herder, Schiller, Mme de Staël, Beethoven, Napoleon, Heine, Carlyle, and Thackeray. It is moreover attractively illustrated.

For a sampling of Goethe's writings and opinions, two collections are available: *The Permanent Goethe*, edited by Thomas Mann (New York, 1948) and containing new verse translations by Stephen Spender as well as materials not hitherto translated; and *Goethe: Wisdom and Experience*, edited by Ludwig Curtius and Hermann J. Weigand (New York, 1949). These prose selections from diaries, letters, book reviews, etc., give an insight into Goethe's philosophy of science, politics, love, marriage, and kindred topics.

The important critical essays of which Goethe has formed the subject would alone fill a large bookcase. The student might well begin with those written by Carlyle in the *Foreign Review* for 1828 and reprinted in his *Collected Essays*. Owing to Byron's place in the Romanticist world and Goethe's interest in him, the comparative essay "Byron and Goethe," by Joseph Mazzini (Scott Library, London, n.d.), should itself be compared with a modern scholar's treatment of the same pair, "Goethe and Byron," by E. M. Butler (Nottingham, 1949), and then with Arnold Bergstraesser's comprehensive treatment of *Goethe's Image of Man and Society* (Chicago, 1949).

At this point the field is open to adventure in many

directions. Two important though very brief volumes may suggest lines to follow: Ernst Cassirer's *Rousseau, Kant, Goethe* (Princeton, 1945) and C. R. Buxton's *Prophets of Heaven and Hell: Virgil, Dante, Milton, Goethe* (New York, 1945). The papers read at the Aspen (Colorado) Convocation in 1949 (*Goethe and the Modern Age*, Chicago, 1950) will inform the student about the diversity of contemporary opinion. This reading may be followed by Albert Schweitzer's two addresses, translated by C. R. Joy and C. T. Campion and published as *Goethe* (Boston, 1949); Karl Viëtor's *Goethe the Poet* (Cambridge, 1949); Thomas Mann's four essays in *Essays of Three Decades*, translated by H. T. Lowe-Porter (New York, 1949); Ernst Robert Curtius's "Goethe as Critic," in *The Hopkins Review*, II, 3 (Summer, 1949); George Santayana, *Three Philosophical Poets* (Anchor edition, 1953); and André Gide's "Goethe," in *Autumn Leaves*, translated by Elsie Pell (New York, 1950).

Finally, the student of Faust proper should be directed to one essay and one book: Lionel Trilling's discussion of the Faust theme in the booklet accompanying the RCA-Victor LP recording of Gounod's *Faust;* and the comprehensive survey of the *Fortunes of Faust*, by E. M. Butler (Cambridge, 1952). Searchers after pictures, autographs, documents, and other primary sources should consult the Goetheana Collection at Yale, as well as others listed in *The Goethe Centuries: 1749–1949*, a useful illustrated catalogue obtainable for seventy-five cents from the Government Printing Office (Washington, D.C., 1950).

J.B.

Foreword to the 1930 Translation

Quiet Work

One lesson, Nature, let me learn of thee,
One lesson which in every wind is blown,
One lesson of two duties kept at one
Though the loud world proclaimed their enmity—

Of toil unsever'd from tranquillity!
Of labour, that in lasting fruit outgrows
Far noisier schemes, accomplish'd in repose,
Too great for haste, too high for rivalry!

Yes, while on earth a thousand discords ring,
Man's fitful uproar mingling with his toil,
Still do thy sleepless ministers move on,

Their glorious tasks in silence perfecting;
Still working, blaming still our vain turmoil,
Labourers that shall not fail, when man is gone.

During the many years in which *Faust* has been my companion, this sonnet of Matthew Arnold's has become more and more closely associated with it. For the poem expresses the temper in which this translation has slowly evolved and also the spirit in which Goethe toiled to understand Nature, but to which he gave expression only in the second part of *Faust*. The significance of Goethe's labor, which "in lasting fruit outgrows far noisier schemes," can be more clearly understood as we approach the hundredth year following his death than during his lifetime.

Today every nation which bears the imprint of Western culture acknowledges Goethe's influence, and gradually the world has come to realize his pre-eminence as a human being, that he is in truth "the first full-statured man," as

Bayard Taylor so happily expressed it. Goethe is so important to modern man because he struggled consciously and ceaselessly throughout his life to integrate the manifold aspects of his richly endowed personality under the hierarchy of his will; his conflicts were struggles which led to self-mastery, his aim the development of his possibilities, and his goal the conquest of his own nature.

There has come into existence a Goethe-world, and one of the happiest experiences of the past years has been the communicating and sharing of this translation with kindred spirits. To many friends who have shared the trials and tribulations of the Faustian pilgrimage my thanks are due.

It gives me great pleasure to acknowledge the assistance of Richard Bloch, whose lifelong study of Faust enabled him to render such signal service to the translation in its earlier stages, and of Alice Rodewald, whose scholarly criticism clarified many a problem in English prosody.

But, above all, this translation is indebted to the late Professor William A. Speck of Yale University for his never-failing aid and encouragement as the work emerged into its final form. Only because of his unsparing generosity and devotion to the exactness of the original have I been able to learn the lesson of "two duties kept at one," and to bring the art of the poet into harmony with the demands of the scholar. Under Professor Speck's guidance, in the quiet of the Goethe room, during many hours of "toil unsever'd from tranquillity," this translation slowly ripened into maturity and now stands as an acknowledgment to his labor of love.

ALICE RAPHAEL

May 15, 1930

Mrs. Raphael's 1930 translation of *Faust: Part I* was published in the following editions:

1930—With an Introduction for the Modern Reader by Mark Van Doren and woodcuts by Lynd Ward. Jonathan Cape & Harrison Smith.

1932—With an Introduction by Carl F. Schreiber and a Note by Mark Van Doren; illustrations by René Clark. The Limited Editions Club.

1939 and 1951—With an Introduction by Carl F. Schreiber and a Note by Mark Van Doren; illustrations by Eugène Delacroix. Heritage Press.

Foreword to the 1955 Translation

The lone being can accomplish little, but he who unites himself with others at the right moment can accomplish much.
—Goethe: *The Parable*

In this foreword, I wish to express my appreciation to a widening circle of Faust friends, for the translation, first published in 1930, did not remain static; and at the same time I should like to afford my readers a glimpse into the unique individuality of the late William A. Speck, founder of the Goethe Museum at Yale University, with which I have been closely identified for many years. Unfortunately, Mr. Speck did not live to see the translation he had sponsored; and, still sadder to relate, he died in 1928 knowing only that plans were in the making to establish, in its handsome permanent quarters in the new Sterling Memorial Library, the great collection of Goetheana which he had begun to build up in early manhood.

Mr. Speck had been compelled to renounce his earnest desire to become a professor of chemistry, and he returned at once, upon his graduation from college, to the little town of Haverstraw on the Hudson, there to assist his father in his apothecary. There began his years of apprenticeship to Goethe. The years of his mastership began when he was nearing fifty. He was already known to the heads of the archives of Weimar and of Frankfort-on-the-Main as a scholarly collector when he gave his collection to Yale University and became a permanent staff member of the library there. He edited many of his valuable manuscripts, he widened the outlying areas of the collection, and he gave courses on Goethe in the graduate school. He told me once that on the day of his first lecture he felt that he had now become the man he had so earnestly desired to be in early life—a teacher. Under Mr. Speck's guidance I learned to meet the demands established once for all time by Bayard Taylor. These standards, set during the Victorian era, implied that no single line could be added and none subtracted; the strictest discipline had to be maintained in wrestling with the essential meaning of words. Mr. Speck also convinced me of the wisdom of bringing my translation as close as possible to the "metrical arrangement of the original," although at the same time he encouraged my resolution to achieve a version that would meet the demands both of the modern reader and of the modern stage.

Goethe himself found pleasure in the art of translation and, at the peak of his career in 1805, he translated the autobiography of Benvenuto Cellini. He spoke of the art of translation to Eckermann, with whom he conversed on so many subjects, on February 9, 1831, when he said:

Nowadays technicalities are everything, and critics begin to torment themselves whether in a rhyme an *S* should be followed by an *S*, and not an *S* by a "double *S*." If I were young and bold enough I would purposely offend against all these technical whims; I would employ alliteration, assonance, false rhyme, and anything else that came into my head, but I would keep the main point in view, and endeavour to say such good things that everyone would be tempted to read them and to learn them by heart.

I kept my main point ever in view; namely, that despite the rigors of scholarship the eventual rendering must emerge not only as a readable book but also as an actable drama. Under Mr. Speck's tutelage I learned to appreciate, as never before, the groundwork training of literary scholarship, analogous to that of pure science. But I learned also what he meant when he said, "I care most of all for a good rendering of a poet's meaning."

Shortly after the death of Mr. Speck, Dr. Carl F. Schreiber, Leavenworth Professor of German Literature at

Yale, was made curator of the Goethe Museum. Thanks to Dr. Schreiber's thoughtful guidance, the museum now ranks with the archives at Frankfort-on-the-Main and at Weimar, and with the collection of Anton Kippenberg, which is to be established as a national museum at Düsseldorf. Only at Yale, moreover, is personal assistance offered to the student who is interested in furthering a project of his own. This is true whether the student is interested in any phase of Goethe's manifold writings or in the literature of the baroque period preceding Goethe's birth in 1749. To round out the Goethe Museum, Dr. Schreiber arranged the incorporation of a great collection of books brought to this country from Munich shortly after the advent of Hitler. This is the unique collection of baroque literature assembled by Dr. Curt Faber von Faur.

With a generosity equal to that of his predecessor, Dr. Schreiber made me at once welcome, and I have continued to go to New Haven almost every week, to meet with him and report upon my work from 1929 to this day. It was he who urged me, in 1943, to revise my 1930 translation, and he assisted me in reworking many passages during the ensuing years. To my dismay, upon the completion of this task I found that I had not yet achieved that perfected form to which Goethe alluded in The Prologue in the Theater, written twenty-seven or -eight years after he had begun to occupy himself with the Faust legend. Speaking through the character of the Poet, Goethe said:

> Often the perfect form appears
> Only when ripened slowly many years.
> What glitters lives an instant, then is gone;
> The real for all posterity lives on.

I now turned to my friend, Mrs. Mary Senior Churchill, whose keen sense of poetic values was a factor of inestimable assistance at this juncture. A small residue of metrical problems was later placed before Professor Mark Van Doren of Columbia University, my neighbor and friend, who had written the introduction to the first edition. When he had passed judgment upon a moot point in prosody, I rested content. Professor William S. Haas, formerly Professor of Philosophy at the University of Cologne, and latterly of Columbia University, gave me his help in a number of questions of interpretation. After arrangements had been made to publish my revised translation in Rinehart Editions, my friend Miss Katherine Thaxter gave me her deft assistance in solving some additional problems of metrics. Professor Jacques Barzun of Columbia, who wrote the introduction to this edition, made a number of valuable suggestions, as did the editorial staff of Rinehart & Company, Inc.

The taboo against stage productions of *Faust: Part I* was broken in 1938 when Max Reinhardt produced it in a vast open-air performance at the Pilgrimage Theatre in Los Angeles, for which the 1930 version of my translation was chosen. In 1949, when Yale celebrated the Goethe Bicentennial, as did nearly all universities in this country, I had the pleasure of seeing my translation produced by the School of Drama under the sponsorship of the Department of German. Two days later it was produced by the Dramatic Association of Oberlin College.

Before closing I wish to encourage students of today to try out their literary gifts and skills in the oft-neglected art of translation, bidding them remember that it is far more important to have power in their own language than to be fluent in a second tongue; for knowledge of a second language can always be gained if one has a solid base upon which to build. I wish also to implant this idea in the mind of the student who would try his wings in translation: do not choose your subject by a purely intellectual process, but let yourself be guided by a genuine identification with the original work. It may be something in German remembered from a childhood in Pennsylvania or St. Louis or Milwaukee; it may be a French tale remembered from Quebec or the Canadian border country; it may be a Spanish or Italian poem brought here by your ancestors; it may be a work you learned about in your high school Latin class or in your military service in Korea. Whatever it may be, let it come to you upon the winged feet of inspiration, but be sure that you are ready to give it the loving care that it deserves.

In taking a final leave of this translation, I should like to quote three lines from Goethe's dedication to *Faust*, written seven years after the first publication of the drama in 1790:

> Life's labyrinthine, wavering course I see:
> Calling to mind the friends by fate deprived
> Of happy years, who thus were lost to me.

To my good fortune, many friends have not been lost but will share with me the completion of a life task. To these friends—the absent and the present—I dedicate this revised edition.

ALICE RAPHAEL

Washington, Conn.
July 1, 1955

Contents

FAUST: *A Tragedy, Part I*

Dedication

Once more you come, wavering forms who passed
In earlier days before my troubled sight.
This once shall I attempt to hold you fast?
In that illusion do I still delight?
Out of mists and shadows you awaken,
And crowd about me! Come then, take full sway,
For, as in youth, my being is shaken
By breath of magic which round you seems to play.

A vision of happier days you now unveil,
And wraiths of friends once dear to me arise;   10
As in an ancient, half-forgotten tale,
First love and friendship pass before my eyes
Through plaintive echoes sorrow is revived,
Life's labyrinthine, wavering course I see,
Calling to mind the friends by fate deprived
Of happy years, who thus were lost to me.

They do not hear the songs which follow still,
Those souls to whom I gave my earliest song;
Forever scattered is the friendly throng,
Alas! that first response, now mute and chill!   20
By many unknown to me my voice is heard,
Whose very praise intimidates my heart;
And they whom once my song so deeply stirred,
If living still, are scattered far apart.

Unwonted yearning stirs in me desire
For that untroubled spirit-realm today;
My trembling song, faint as an Aeolian lyre,

1

Quavers unsteadily, then dies away.
A shudder seizes me! Tears follow tears,
My austere heart grows tender, and I feel   30
What I possess far, far away appears;
Now the vanished life alone seems real.

The Prologue in the Theater

MANAGER   DRAMATIC POET   COMIC CHARACTER

MANAGER

You two, who often stood by me
In days of trouble and of need,
Tell me, whether in Germany
Our undertaking will succeed?
I want to please the crowd we get,
Because it lives and lets us live; each seat
Is taken, our booth is up, the stage is set,
And everyone is waiting for a treat.
Already in their places, with eyebrows raised,
They sit composed and want to be amazed.   10
The public I know how to interest,
But into such a fix I've ne'er been led:
It's true they're not accustomed to the best,
Yet what a frightful quantity they've read!
How shall we ever make things fresh and new,
Contain a meaning, yet be pleasing too?
Frankly it pleases me to see the throng
As toward our booth it streams along
And, by incessant surging swept apace,
Presses through the narrow gate of Grace.   20
By daylight, even ere the hour of four,
Crowding the ticket window they start to row;
As folk in famine storm the baker's door
They almost break their necks for tickets now.
The poet's miracle alone can sway
Such various minds. O friend, do this today!

3

POET

Oh, speak not of that motley throng—
One glance compels my spirit into flight!
Veil from me the crowd which whirls along
And sucks us in the vortex 'gainst our will!   30
No! lead me to a nook divinely still,
Wherein the poet alone finds pure delight,
Where love and friendship with divine control
Create and train the gifts of heart and soul.
What from our deepest being seemed to course,
What bashful lips tried shyly to express,
Sometimes with failure, sometimes with success,
Is swallowed by a violent moment's force.
Often the perfected form appears
Only when ripened slowly many years.   40
What glitters lives an instant, then is gone;
The real for all posterity lives on.

COMIC CHARACTER

Posterity? That word offends my ears!
Suppose *I* talked of future years,
Who would amuse the world today?
They want and ought to have their fun;
A lad of spirit in your play
Has value too, when all is said and done.
The public's moods will never irritate
The man who gives his best with charm and ease;   50
He'll long for larger crowds to animate,
To rouse and sway as he may please.
Cheer up, and show what you can do!
Let Phantasy with all her train appear,
Bring Feeling, Reason, Sense and Passion here,
But, listen to me—not without Folly too!

MANAGER

Especially give action its full share!
They come to gaze and they prefer to stare.
If only you will reel off all you can,
And make the wond'ring crowd gape with delight,   60
Then the goal is virtually in sight,
And you will be a very popular man.
The masses by mass alone an author swings,
Each one eventually selects his fare;
He who brings much, something to many brings,
And each one leaves contented with his share.
If giving a piece, give it in pieces now!
Such hash I'm sure you can prepare;
Easy to give, it's easily invented;
Why bother with a whole, when what's presented,   70
The public will pick to pieces anyhow!

POET

How base such hack-work is! Do you not feel
It is unworthy of an artist's soul?
You've made a virtue which you would extol
Out of the stuff and nonsense in which you deal.

MANAGER

Rebukes of that sort don't offend:
A serious worker must depend
Upon the tools which he considers good.
Remember that you have to split soft wood!
Just look about—whom are you writing for?   80
This fellow comes as bored as bored can be,
Another comes who dined too heavily,
And frankly, what I most abhor,
Some from reading the papers run to me.
Heedless, they rush to us, as to a masquerade,

Spurred on by curiosity alone:
The ladies perform a part yet are not paid,
Showing off in all the finery they own.
What do you dream of in your poet's sphere?
How does a crowded house affect your mood?   90
Study your patrons well, draw near,
Half are indifferent, half are rude!
One wants a game of cards after the play,
Another a wanton for the night.
Why then, poor fools, annoy and pray
The Muses for an end so trite?
I tell you, give them more—more than they ever ask:
Then from your goal you cannot go far wrong.
Attempt to mystify the throng;
To satisfy is far too hard a task.   100
What ails you—is it elation or disgust?

POET

Go, seek another slave! Oh, must
The poet take the highest gift we know,
The human gift which Nature did bestow,
And squander it upon a wanton show?
How does he stir all hearts, and how control
The elements? Is it not by harmony of soul
He draws the world into his heart again?
When round the distaff Nature winds
With unconcern the thread of life,   110
And when discordant beings of all kinds,
Twisted together, clash in cruel strife,
Infusing life, who makes the separation
By which they fall in order rhythmically?
Who unifies and brings to consecration
Parts of the whole, creating harmony?
Who makes the tempest rage with passionate wrath?
Who makes you feel the glowing sunset hours?

Who scatters the fairest springtime flowers
Over the Belovèd's path?   120
Who twines the laurel wreath with simple rites,
Merit in every field to glorify?
Who makes Olympus safe? the gods unites?
The power of man, which poets personify!

COMIC CHARACTER

Then use the powers by which you're swayed
To carry on the poet trade,
Much as you would some love affair.
By chance you meet, are stirred, you linger there,
And little by little you are involved;
Joy waxes, then it is dissolved,   130
Rapture comes first, grief will next advance,
And, ere you know it, you have a real romance.
Let's also try to give a play like this;
Probe the depths of life, its pain, its bliss.
Each lives it, although understood by few;
It's full of interest wherever grasped by you.
With varicolored pictures—not too clear—
Much error and a spark of truth,
The best drink will be brewed to cheer
And edify the world. Then youth   140
In all its fairest flower will arrive,
And as a revelation hail your play;
While sentimental natures will derive
Their melancholy food from what you say.
First at this and then at that they'll start,
As each perceives what's buried in his heart.
They come prepared to laugh or cry with ease,
Pathos they applaud, illusion they adore;
Who deems himself complete is hard to please,
A maturing soul is grateful evermore.   150

POET

Then give me back those years long past
When I could still mature and grow,
And when a spring of song welled fast
Out of my heart with ceaseless flow,
When all the world was veiled in mist,
When every bud a miracle concealed,
And when I gathered myriad flowers
Crowding the valley and the field.
Though naught was mine, I had enough in youth,
A joy in illusion, a longing for the Truth.   160
Give back the surge of impulse, re-create
That happiness so steeped in pain,
The power of love, the strength of hate—
Oh, give me back my youth again!

COMIC CHARACTER

Youth, my friend, beyond a doubt you'll need
When enemies in combat press,
Or when lovely creatures plead
Ardently for your caress,
When the victor's wreath, from a distant site,
Lures you to a difficult goal unwon,   170
When, feasting and drinking, you pass the night,
After a frenzied dance and wanton fun.
To strike the well-known cords with strength,
With courage and with animation,
While to a self-appointed goal at length
You ramble with pleasant deviation—
That, aged sirs, should be your task today,
And we esteem you for it none the less.
Age does not make us childish, as they say,
But finds us children still, I must confess!   180

MANAGER

Sufficient words have been exchanged—
Let us have action move apace!
While compliments are thus arranged,
Something useful could be taking place.
Why talk of inspiration when
It never comes to people who delay!
If you claim to be a poet, then
Command the Muse of Poetry to obey!
You know quite well what we require,
Let's sip strong drink with spark and fire.   190
Brew it at once, it's time it was begun!
What's not done now, tomorrow won't be done.
Let not one single day slip past,
Let resolution then be bold,
Clasping occasion by the forelock fast,
And since it must—and won't let go its hold—
It labors stanchly to the last.
Upon our German stage you know
Each tries out what he wants to see;
So don't be stingy putting on your show,   200
With either props or scenery.
Use the heavenly lights, the great and small,
Scatter the stars with a lavish hand;
Water, fire, and rocky wall,
Birds and beasts are all at your command.
Thus in our narrow booth today,
Creation's ample scope display;
And wander swiftly, yet observing well,
From Heaven through the world to Hell.

The Prologue in Heaven

THE ALMIGHTY   THE HEAVENLY HOST
Afterward MEPHISTOPHELES

The THREE ARCHANGELS *step forward*

RAPHAEL

The sun is chanting his ancient song
In contest with the brother spheres,
Rolling with thunder steps along,
Down the predestined course of years.
His presence gives the angels might,
Though fathom it none ever may;
And Thy sublime works still are bright
With splendor of Creation's day.

GABRIEL

And swift and ever swifter swings
The world with glory into sight, 10
And heavenly light on golden wings
Yields to the shuddering depths of night;
In foaming waves the sea is flung
Against the rocks with swirling force,
And rock and sea are pulled and swung
Into the spheres' eternal course.

MICHAEL

And storms an angry struggle wage
From sea to land, from land to sea,
Forging a mighty chain in rage
Of ever-flowing energy. 20

Beyond lies blazing desolation
Where crashing thunder flames its way;
Thy heralds, though, in adoration
Revere Thy gently changing day.

THE THREE TOGETHER

This vision gives the angels might,
Though fathom it none ever may;
And all Thy lofty works are bright
With splendor of Creation's day.

MEPHISTOPHELES

Since you, O Lord, once more are drawing near
To question us how matters seem to be, 30
Since once it pleased you seeing me—well, here
Amongst these lackeys—gaze on me!
Excuse me, but I can't be eloquent,
Not even though I'm scorned by all your staff;
My pathos would provoke your merriment,
Had you not quite forgotten how to laugh.
Of suns and worlds I've not one word to say,
How men torment themselves is all I see.
That little earth-god stays the same eternally,
And is as odd as on Creation's day. 40
He would be better off, in life at least,
Had you withheld from him the spark of heavenly light;
He calls it reason, using it as his right
To be more animal than a beast.
Saving your gracious presence, he seems to me
Like a lanky grasshopper which ceaselessly
Flies about and flying springs,
Then back in the grass the same old ditty sings.
Were he but satisfied as in the grass he lies!
But no, he digs his nose in all the dirt he spies. 50

THE ALMIGHTY

Have you nothing more to say?
Must you endlessly complain?
Is nothing ever right on earth?

MEPHISTOPHELES

No, Lord, life is as rotten as before!
I pity men, in misery from birth;
I even hate to plague them any more.

THE ALMIGHTY

Do you know Faust?

MEPHISTOPHELES

The Doctor?

THE ALMIGHTY

And my servant!

MEPHISTOPHELES

Indeed he serves you in a curious fashion!   60
No earthly food and drink allays his passion;
An inner ferment drives him far,
Yet of his frenzy he's but half aware.
From heaven he demands the fairest star,
From earth all joys supremely rare,
Yet neither what is near nor what is far
Can ease the deep disturbance of his breast.

THE ALMIGHTY

Although he serves me now confusedly,
I soon will lead him where the light is clear.
The Gardener knows, when fresh green tips the tree,   70
That flower and fruit will deck the coming year!

MEPHISTOPHELES

What will you bet? That man you're bound to lose,
If—with your permission—I may lead
Him lightly into my path, and as I choose!

THE ALMIGHTY

As long as he remains on earth—agreed!
Nothing is forbidden you contrive;
Man errs as long as he doth strive.

MEPHISTOPHELES

Thank you! Frankly, for the dead
I never hankered much; instead
I'd rather have a cheek quite plump and red.   80
I'm out if ever a corpse comes to my house;
I act just as a cat does with a mouse.

THE ALMIGHTY

So be it, it is your affair!
Divert this spirit from its primal source,
And, if you can catch him, drag him where
You go upon your downward course;
And stand ashamed, at last forced to admit:
Man, in essence good, though darkly driven,
Knows in himself the Right and the way to it.

MEPHISTOPHELES

Agreed! I'll make short work of it!   90
As regards my wager I've no fear.
And when I reach my goal, you must permit
That, puffed with triumph, I may venture here!
Dust shall he eat, and with gusto, too,
As my relative the snake was wont to do.

THE ALMIGHTY

Here, too, you have a free hand openly;
I never have abhorred your sort and kind.
Of all denying spirits known to me,
Least does the waggish knave offend my mind.
Too quickly stilled is man's activity,   100
Too soon he longs for unconditioned rest;
Hence I bestowed this comrade willingly,
Who goads and, as a devil, creates best.
But ye, God's own true Sons, enjoy and bless
Life and its abundant loveliness.
May the creative and eternal might
Clasp you in bonds which lofty love has wrought,
May that which fluctuates in drifting light
Be fortified by permanence of thought!

(*The Heavens close;* the ARCHANGELS *separate.*)

MEPHISTOPHELES (*alone*)

I like to meet the Chief from time to time;   110
And watch my step on cordial terms to stay.
How kind of such a dignitary to chat
Even with the Devil, in this human way!

First Part of the Tragedy

I

NIGHT

A narrow high-vaulted Gothic room; Faust *sits restlessly in his armchair at his desk.*

FAUST

I've studied all Philosophy,
Medicine and Jurisprudence too,
Even, to my grief, Theology
With fervent efforts through and through,
Yet here I stand, poor fool! what's more,
No whit wiser than before!
I'm Master, Doctor, and I've found
For ten long years, that as I chose
I led my students by the nose,
First up, then down, then all around,   10
To see that nothing can be known!
This cuts me to the quick, I'll own!
I'm cleverer than all that tribe—
Doctor, Lawyer, Parson, Scribe.
All doubts and scruples I dispel,
I have no fear of Devil or Hell,
Wherefore I'm shorn of joy as well.
I don't think much of what I know,
I don't imagine I could show
Men how they could mend their ways,   20
Or help them on to better days.
Not even property or gold,

15

Or worldly honors do I hold!
No dog would stand this any more!
Wherefore I've turned to magic lore,
So that through lips of spirits, and force,
Many a secret to its source
I'll trace, and need no longer sweat and grieve
To teach what I do not believe.
So I'll discover what it is that binds   30
The world together, so that I'll find
The forces stirring in the seed,
And from spinning empty words be freed.

O glowing moon, didst thou but shine
A last time on this pain of mine!
Behind this desk how oft have I
At midnight seen thee rising high!
O'er books and papers when I'd bend,
Thou didst appear, O mournful friend!
Ah, could I on mountain height,   40
Roam in thy softly tender light,
O'er the fields at twilight trail,
Drifting with spirits of hill and dale;
Then freed from knowledge and its pain,
Bathed in thy dew, my health regain.

Alas! am I still penned in alone?
Damnable dungeon walls of stone,
Where even the tender light of heaven wanes
Drearily through the painted window panes!
Hemmed in by a toppling, dusty mound   50
Of worm-eaten volumes without end
Which up to the vaulted arch extend
With sooty papers fastened around?
With glasses and boxes, crammed and packed,
And instruments together hurled,

Ancestral stuff, heaped up and stacked—
That is my world! And what a world!

Do you then wonder why your heart
Beats anxiously within your breast,
Why an unexplainable pain and smart   60
Clogs the flow of life and zest?
Instead of Nature's quickened sphere
Into which man by God was thrust,
Skeletons surround you here
Of beasts and men, in mold and dust.

Be off! Away! To broad, free lands!
This volume wherein mysteries hide,
From Nostradamus'* very hand,
Is not this book sufficient guide?
Then the course of stars you'll learn,   70
And Nature, teaching you, will inflate
Your soul with power, then you'll discern
How spirits with spirits communicate.
All this dry pondering is in vain
The holy symbols to explain.
Ye hover, spirits, near me . . . near.
Answer me, if you can hear!

(*He opens the book and gazes upon the sign of the
Macrocosm.*)

Ha! at this one burning glance what ecstasy
Courses through my senses once again!
I feel a youthful holy joy of life,   80
Quivering through every nerve and vein!
Was it a god who wrote this sign, which stills

---

* Michel de Notredame (1503–1566), a noted French physician and astrologer who published a book of rimed prophecies still in circulation today.

Ⓧ My inner tumult, fills
My troubled heart with joy,
And with mysterious force reveals
The power of Nature which about me steals?
Am I a god? My spirit grows so clear!
I gaze on these pure hieroglyphs and here,
Bared to my soul, Nature at work I feel!
At last I understand the sage who said,   90
"The World of Spirits is not barred to thee;
Thy mind is sealed, thy heart is dead!
Up, student! bathe unweariedly
Thy earthly breast in morning-red."

(*He contemplates the sign.*)

How toward the Whole all things are blending,
Each in the other living, growing!
How heavenly forces, soaring, descending,
Are in and out of golden buckets flowing,
While fragrant blessings, lightly winging
From heaven through the earth, are bringing   100
Harmonies which through the Whole are ringing!

What a pageant! But, alas, only a show!
Where shall I grasp thee, illimitable Nature?
Where, ye breasts! from which all life doth flow,
To which my withered soul must strive?
Earth and heavens ye sustain,
Ye flow, ye nourish—yet must I long in vain?

(*He turns over the pages of the book impatiently and perceives the sign of the* EARTH-SPIRIT.)

How differently I'm affected by this sign!
Thou, Spirit of Earth, art nearer me;
Already I feel the surge of energy,   110
Already I feel suffused as if with wine.

I feel new strength to face the world again,
To endure all earthly joy, all earthly pain,
To battle through all storms with might and main,
From crashing shipwreck rise and still attain.
Clouds are gathering . . .
The moon conceals her light . . .
The lamp is flickering low!
Mists rise—red flashes, swift and bright,
Play about my head! A chilling breath   120
Creeps downward from the vaulted roof
Gripping me fast!
I feel thee hovering near, O Spirit oft invoked!
Reveal thyself at last!
Ah, how my beating heart is choked!
With new emotions
My senses are made rife!
I feel that all my heart goes out to thee!
Thou must! thou must! although it cost my life!

(*He seizes the book and pronounces mysteriously the invocation of the* EARTH-SPIRIT. *A reddish flame bursts forth, and the* SPIRIT *appears in the flame.*)

SPIRIT

Who calls?   130

FAUST (*turning away*)

O terrifying face!

SPIRIT

With compelling power thou hast drawn me here:
And long hast thou drawn sustenance from my sphere,
Yet now—

FAUST

Oh, I cannot endure thee!

SPIRIT

Breathlessly didst come—to gaze on me,
To hear my voice, my countenance to see;
To the powerful yearning of thy soul I bow.
Here, then, am I!—What pitiable horror now
Grips thee, superior one! Where are the soul's outcries,   140
The heart which from its depths a world created,
Bore and cherished it—then by ecstasy dilated,
To us the spirits sought at once to rise?
Where art thou, Faust, whose voice rang in my ears,
Who toward me pressed with overwhelming might?
Art *thou* he, who in my breath's atmosphere,
A writhing, crumpled worm appears—
Trembling to the marrow in his fright?

FAUST

Creature of flame, why should I flinch before thee?
Yes, it is Faust, thy equal, I am he!   150

SPIRIT

In the tides of life, in action's storm,
Rising, sinking, I flow
To and fro!
Birth and death to me
An eternal sea,
A changing and weaving,
Life glowing and seething;
Thus toiling at the humming loom of time and fate,
The Godhead's living vestures I create.

FAUST

Thou who dost embrace the universe,   160
Creative Spirit, how similar we are!

SPIRIT

Thou resemblest the Spirit thou canst understand—
Not me!

(*Disappears.*)

FAUST (*overwhelmed*)

Not thee?
Whom then?
I, image of the Godhead!
And not like thee?

(*A knock*)

God's Death! I know that knock—my famulus!
This means an end to my delight!
Why must that shriveled grind destroy   170
My glorious vision at its height!

(*Enter* WAGNER *in a dressing gown and a nightcap, a lamp
in his hand.* FAUST *turns to him with annoyance.*)

WAGNER

Pardon me, I heard you declaiming a part;
Reading a Grecian tragedy, no doubt?
I'd like to gain more practice in this art,
As nowadays it helps one out.
I've often heard it said, a preacher
Does well to take an actor as a teacher.

FAUST

Yes, if the preacher is inclined
To be an actor, as you sometimes find.

WAGNER

Immured within a study, how can men   180
Who scarcely ever see the world, and then
Only from afar as through a telescope,
To guide it by persuasion ever hope?

FAUST

Unless you feel it, great efforts are in vain.
Unless this feeling surges from your soul
With primal force of pleasure, to control
Your listeners' hearts—if this you cannot gain,
Just sit forever! Patch and glue each bit,
From someone else's feast concoct a stew,
Puffing the wretched flame you've lit   190
Out of your little ash-heap too!
If to make apes and children gape and start
Is to your taste and all you seek—
Well and good! But words won't link a heart to heart,
Save from your own heart you freely speak.

WAGNER

Elocution makes the orator though;
I feel indeed that I have far to go.

FAUST

Strive for an honorable success!
Be no empty-sounding fool in your address!
Common sense and truth—these do not need   200
Either art or much display;
Why hunt high-sounding words indeed,
If you have something true to say?
Those speeches filled with tinsel words, which try
To fool humanity with childish prattle,
Are lifeless as the misty winds which sigh,
And through the withered leaves in autumn rattle!

WAGNER

Ah, how long is Art,
While Life is brief!
Critical efforts often leave my heart 210
And mind depressed with grief.
How difficult to gain the means whereby
A man may rise and reach the source!
And ere he covers half the given course,
Alas, poor devil, he must die.

FAUST

Is parchment then the sacred spring that pours
A draught which evermore will slake your thirst?
No, no, refreshment never will be yours,
Unless deep from your soul it gushes first.

WAGNER

Pardon! but it is a treat to cast 220
Ourselves into the spirit of the past,
To see what sages formerly expressed,
Then to what noble heights we have progressed.

FAUST

Oh, yes! Unto the stars on high!
The ages of the past, my friend,
Are to us a book of seven seals; what you suspected
To be the spirit of the times, proves in the end
To be your spirit—nothing more—
In which the ages are reflected.
This fact we frequently deplore, 230
And at a first glance, run away.
'Tis but an attic, a rubbish nest,
At most a mere political display,
Pragmatic maxims, phrases in a way
Which suit the mouths of puppets best!

WAGNER

But then the world—man's heart—his soul!
If each could know a portion of the whole!

FAUST

Yes, what one calls knowing! Who dares claim
The right to give the child its own true name?
The few who knew somewhat, who did not shield   240
Their brimming hearts, but foolishly revealed
Their thoughts and feelings to the mob—they always died
At the stake, or else were crucified.
But it is dead of night! Excuse me, friend,
Our conversation now must end.

WAGNER

I would have shared your vigil with delight,
And carried on our learned talk all night.
I'll bring tomorrow—being Easter Day—
These and other questions if I may.
I've studied zealously; yet, though   250
I know so much—still, all I'd like to know.

(*Exit.*)

FAUST (*alone*)

How hope does not abandon such a brain,
To shallow stuff forevermore glued fast;
He digs with greedy hands for hidden gain,
Delighted if he finds a worm at last!

Dare the voice of such a man resound
Here, where the fullness of spirit-life I found?
But, ah! this time my deepest thanks you've won,
Earth's most miserable son!
You snatched me from the dark despondency   260
Which threatened to destroy my mind before.

The vision was stupendous, and I see
I am a dwarf, a dwarf and nothing more!

I, God's image, who already thought
To near the mirror of eternal Truth, who sought
To revel in clarity and heavenly light,
Freed from mortal plight—
I, more than Cherub, whose unbridled force
Presumed to flow through Nature's veins,
And, like the gods creating, sought their planes,   270
How I am punished! From my lofty course
A word of thunder swept me back aghast.

I do not dare compare myself to thee!
I had the power to draw thee close to me,
Yet not the force by which to hold thee fast.
In that holy moment I seemed to be
So little, yet so very great,
Thou didst thrust me cruelly
Back into uncertainties of human fate.
Whose teaching shall I heed? What shall I shun?   280
Shall I obey each inner urge?
Alas! our deeds, as well as sorrows, one by one
Clog the current of our life's deep surge.

To lofty glories which our soul receives,
Strange and stranger substance always cleaves;
When in the good of this world we can share,
We call the better a delusion and a snare;
Whilst noble feelings given us by life
Congeal in a universe of restless strife.

Phantasy on daring pinions in the past,   290
Swelled by hope, sailed into infinite space;
Now she is satisfied with a little place,

Since joy on joy in the whirlpool of time is cast.
Care, lurking deeply in each heart,
There causes many a secret sorrow,
Restlessly driving joy and peace apart;
Disguised with changing masks each morrow,
She appears as house or land, or child or wife,
Or fire, water, poison, steel;
Though nothing happens, dread you always feel,   300
What you never lose, you mourn throughout your life.

Not like the gods—too conscious of this am I!
I am like the worm which, burrowing in the dust
And seeking there its sustenance, is crushed
And buried by a passer-by.

Is it not dust, wherewith these towering walls
With hundred shelves imprison me,
These thousandfold trifles of trash which endlessly
Confine me to these moldering walls?

Here shall I satisfy my need?   310
What though in thousand volumes I should read
That human beings suffered everywhere,
And one perchance was happy, here or there?
Why grin, you hollow skull, except to say
That once your brain, perplexed like mine,
Yearning for Truth, pursued the light of day,
Then in the dusk went wretchedly astray?
Ye instruments, ye jeer at me, I feel,
Cog and circle, cylinder and wheel!
I stood at the door, ye should have been the key;   320
Though fashioned well, ye raised no latch for me.
Unfathomable by light of day,
Nature will permit no one to steal
Her veil; what to your spirit she will not reveal,
With lever and screw you cannot wrest away.

Old instruments, though never used by me,
Because ye served my father ye remained.
Old scrolls, by taint of smoke ye have been stained,
Since first this desk lamp smoldered drearily.
Wiser to have squandered the little I possessed,   330
Than here sit and sweat, by that little oppressed.
All that your ancestors bequeathed to you,
To make it really yours—earn it anew.
What's useless to you is a burden sore,
What each moment creates it uses, nothing more.

Yet why is my glance attracted to that place?
Is that small phial a magnet for my sight?
Why suddenly within me is all as fair and bright
As when moonbeams flutter in a darkling woodland space?

Rare and precious phial, hail to thee,   340
Which now I take down reverently;
In thee I honor both man's wit and art.
Epitome of sleeping essence—thou
Extract of subtle, deadly powers—impart
Thy favor to thy master now!
I look upon thee . . . fainter seems my pain,
I grasp thee . . . and my strivings wane;
My spirit's tide ebbs more and more.
Toward high seas I am being drawn away;
Below the ocean sparkles; a newer day   350
Lures me to another shore!

On delicate pinions drifting hither to me
A fiery chariot nears! Ah, I prepare
To open a new pathway through the air
To newer spheres of purer activity!
This higher life, this godlike bliss,
Do you, but now a worm, deserve all this?
Only be resolute and boldly turn

Your back upon this sunny world! Yes, learn
To fling those portals wide   360
From which men shrink and turn aside!
Lo! the hour has come to prove by deed
That manhood to the Godhead will not cede,
Nor facing the gloomy cave will flinch and sway,
Where phantasies, self-tortured, dwell;
But man will strive toward that passageway
About whose narrow mouth flames all of hell;
Calmly he'll take this step, though none the less
The price may be—the plunge into nothingness!

Now, clear crystal cup, descend from thy place: 370
I take thee from thine ancient leather case,
Thee whom I have not thought of many a year!
Sparkling at ancestral feasts thou didst appear,
Enlivening in turn each solemn guest
As thou wert passed from hand to hand; it was a test
For every drinker, then, in rhyme to tell
The meaning of the pictures graven well,
And at one draught drain thee to the end.
This brings back youthful memories to my heart.
I shall not pass thee now to any friend,   380
Nor shall I test my wit upon thine art.
Here is a juice swift to intoxicate,
Whose brownish fluid fills thy hollow bowl.
Let what I prepare—and choose—now be my fate;
Grant this last drink be, with all my soul,
A festal salutation to the dawn!

(*He puts the goblet to his lips.*)

(*Church bells and choir*)

CHORUS OF THE ANGELS

Christ is arisen!
Joy be to the Mortal
Whom corruptible,
Clinging, inherited   390
Imperfection imprisoned!

FAUST

What vibrant sounds, what voices clear and fair
Withdraw the goblet from my lips with power?
O deep-toned bells, do ye already declare
Easter, with its first most sacred hour?
Ye choirs, sing ye that consoling chant
Which rang one night of death from angels' lips
In certainty of a new covenant?

CHORUS OF THE WOMEN

With balm and with sweet-smelling
Spices we strew,   400
We tended and laid him down,
We who were true;
Now binding, now winding
Pure linen around;
Yet, ah! when we seek him,
Christ is not found.

CHORUS OF THE ANGELS

Christ is ascended!
The Beloved is blest,
Whose afflicting yet strengthening,
Chastening test   410
And trial is ended.

FAUST

Why seek me, prostrate in this dusty cell,
Ye heavenly tones, so powerful yet mild?
Ring out beyond where gentle beings dwell!
Although I lack belief, I hear the tidings well;
The miracle is faith's most treasured child.
I dare not strive toward those spheres
From which such blessed tidings rain;
These tones, familiar since my childhood years,
Are calling me to life again.   420
Long, long ago a kiss of heavenly love
Descended on me during Sabbath rest;
Then bells with mystic meaning chimed above,
Prayer was a fervent joy which filled my breast;
A sweet yet ineffable yearning
Drove me then through forest and through field,
And while my eyes with tears were burning
I felt in me another world revealed.
Of merry, youthful play these anthems sing,
Of freedom and the happiness of spring;   430
Memory with childlike feeling thrusts me away
From this last solemn step of pain.
Ring on, ring on, beloved songs of heaven!
My tears are flowing; earth claims me once again!

CHORUS OF THE DISCIPLES

Has He, the buried One,
Living, exalted Son,
Risen already
To glory on high?
In desire of Becoming.
To creative joy is He nigh?   440
On the breast of earth, suffering,
Ah, here we must lie!

Yearning, He left us,
His followers, below;
Ah, Master, we cry for
The bliss Thou dost know!

CHORUS OF THE ANGELS

Christ has transcended
The womb of Corruption!
Let the bonds of destruction
Be joyfully rended!   450
To those serving through deeds,
Spreading love by their teaching,
Sustaining men in their needs,
Bearing tidings and preaching,
He not only is near,
He is verily here!

II

BEFORE THE CITY GATE

All sorts of villagers come forth on foot.

A NUMBER OF APPRENTICES

Why are you going up that way?

OTHERS

We're going to the Hunters' Lodge on the hill.

THE FIRST

We would rather stroll to the Mill.

ONE APPRENTICE

Take my advice, go to the River Inn today.

ANOTHER APPRENTICE

The road up there is none of the best.

OTHERS

And you?

A THIRD

I'll follow with the rest.

A FOURTH

Come to Burgdorf! There you're bound to find
The prettiest girls, beer of the strongest kind,
And first-class rough-and-tumble sport.   10

A FIFTH

You gay dog, are you itching still
For a third sound licking of that sort?
I won't go there, it makes me ill.

A SERVANT GIRL

No, I'm going back, and right away.

ANOTHER GIRL

We're sure to find him by the poplar tree.

THE FIRST

Well, that's not much joy for me;
He'll stay with you the livelong day,
And dance with you or else with none.
What's there for me in all your fun?

THE OTHER GIRL

He will not be alone today;   20
"I'll bring Curly-Head," I heard him say.

STUDENT

Hell! How those hefty wenches step along!
Brother, let's follow them—make haste!
A biting tobacco, beer good and strong,
And a girl in her Sunday best tickles my taste.

A CITIZEN'S DAUGHTER

Look at those handsome fellows, please!
What a shame! Why, they could be
Running with the best society,
Instead of after servant girls like these!

A SECOND STUDENT (*to the first*)

Not quite so fast! Two are coming behind   30
So nicely dressed—and what is more,
One of them is my young neighbor next door!
I've a yen for the girl, and you will find,
Although they walk primly and seem so sedate,
They won't mind if we pick them up . . . hmm, just
    you wait!

THE FIRST STUDENT

Brother, *no!* I'm not easy to faze, I confess!
Hurry, lest these birds make a clean get-away!
The hand which was plying the broom Saturday
Is ready on Sunday with eager caress.

A CITIZEN

No, I don't like him, the new Burgomaster.   40
Since he is in office, his pride grows the faster;
Really, just what does he do for the town?
Are not conditions steadily worse?
We obey and obey, till our life is a curse,
And taxes are more than we ever paid down.

A BEGGAR (*singing*)

Kind sirs, fair ladies, whom I see
With rosy cheeks and handsome dress,
Be good enough to look at me!
Oh, look and lessen my distress!
Oh, let me not strum on in vain!   50
Only the generous are gay.
Since all men celebrate this day,
May it be for me a harvest gain!

ANOTHER CITIZEN

On Sundays and holidays I like nothing more
Than to talk about war and war preparation;
While way off in Turkey, or another far nation,
The masses are fighting as ever before.
One looks out the window and, sipping a glass,
Watches the bright vessels glide down the river.
At nightfall one feels contented to pass   60
Homeward, blessing peace and our era forever.

THIRD CITIZEN

Yes, neighbor, I'm quite in agreement with you.
Let 'em crack their skulls to the end of their days,
Let all go to pot, their scheming fall through!
But at home we will stick to our old-fashioned ways.

AN OLD WOMAN (*to the* CITIZEN'S DAUGHTER)

My, how dressed up! So young and so fair!
Who would not be just mad over you?
Don't be stuck up! No harm's meant, I swear!
And what you want most, I can get you that too!

THE CITIZEN'S DAUGHTER

Come away, Agatha! It's really not right   70
To be seen in broad daylight with such a witch-wife!

Although she did show me last St. Andrew's Night
The man I'm to marry, as if true to life.

THE OTHER GIRL

She showed me mine too, in her clear crystal ball;
There he stood with his comrades—a soldierly man;
Though I keep my eyes open and search where I can,
I've never yet met him, in spite of it all.

THE SOLDIERS

Castles with battlement,
Turrets and tower;
Maidens with arrogant   80
Notions of power,
I would obtain!
Bold is the struggle,
Mighty the gain!

Let trumpets be sounding
As we go by,
Whether to pleasure,
Or whether to die.
O what a tempest!
O what a life!   90
Castles and women
Must yield in such strife.
Bold is the struggle,
Mighty the gain,
As all the soldiers
Go marching amain.

(*Enter* FAUST *and* WAGNER)

FAUST

From icy bondage streams and brooks are freed
By Spring's life-giving, lovely light;

In the valleys hope and happiness swell the seed,
While weak old Winter, creeping out of sight,   100
Back to the rugged mountains must proceed.
From there, still hastening his swift retreat,
He scatters impotent showers of hail and sleet
In furrows o'er the fields of dawning green.
The sun suffers no whiteness to be seen,
When creation surges to form itself everywhere;
The sun would brighten all with color and grace,
But flowers failing, the countryside still bare,
People in holiday garments take their place.
Turn around, and from this height look down   110
Backward on the little town.
See how the motley crowd, with one accord,
Surges from the hollow, gloomy gate!
Each suns himself with joy to celebrate
The resurrection of the Lord.
'Tis they are resurrected from their past,
From dingy rooms in shabby houses cast,
From bondage to their trade, by toil harassed,
From crowded street and narrow alleyway,
From oppressive roofs and gables gray,   120
From the church's sacred night,
All are guided to the light.
Look! How nimbly the crowds below
Scatter in the fields and gardens to and fro,
And how upon the river sway
Many little vessels gay
Whilst, almost sinking 'neath its load,
The last skiff pushes out of sight.
Even from the distant mountain road,
The colored raiment flashes bright.   130
Nearer does the village turmoil rise,
This is truly the people's paradise!
Here great and small revel contentedly;
Here I am human—here human I can be!

WAGNER

Doctor, to take a walk with you
Is an honor and of value too:
But here alone I would not care to be,
For I detest vulgarity.
This shrieking, fiddling, skittling around
Is a most obnoxious sound;   140
They shout as if the Fiend possessed the throng,
And call it pleasure, call it song!

PEASANTS UNDER THE LINDEN TREE

A song and a dance

In his best for the dance, the young shepherd was dressed,
With jacket and sash and a gay-colored vest,
Wreath and ribbons a-flying;
While round the linden each lass with her lad,
Round and round the linden were dancing like mad.
Hurrah! Tra-la-la!
Tra-la-la! Hurrah, rah!
The fiddle and bow were sighing.   150

He pushed and shoved himself into the crowd,
Nudging a young wench who then screamed aloud
As his elbow kept a-plying;
The lively young creature turned round right away,
And said: "You're a nuisance, that's what *I* say!"
Hurrah! Tra-la-la!
Tra-la-la! Hurrah, rah!
"You're a rude one, no denying!"

They flew round the circle with footsteps so light,
They danced to the left, they danced to the right,   160
All petticoats a-flying;
They soon grew so red, they soon grew so warm,

Breathless they paused, arm linked in arm.
Hurrah! Tra-la-la!
Tra-la-la! Hurrah, rah!
Elbow on hip a-lying.

"Now don't you make free quite so fast," said the maid;
"How many a girl has been sadly betrayed
With coaxing and with lying!"
Yet soon he had wheedled her off to one side,   170
While round about the linden, from far and wide,
Hurrah! Tra-la-la!
Tra-la-la! Hurrah! rah!
Came shrieks and the fiddle sighing.

AN OLD PEASANT

Doctor, you are really very kind
To mix with us and not feel proud;
You, so learned a person, do not mind
Strolling midst this pushing crowd.
Accept our choicest jug, today
With cool sweet wine it has been filled;   180
I offer it and wish to say,
Not only may your thirst be stilled,
But may your life span ever gain
Days many as the drops this cup contains.

FAUST

I accept the drink, and gladly too;
Good health to one and all of you.

(*The people form a circle about him.*)

THE OLD PEASANT

To tell the truth, that you appear
Upon a holiday seems only right;

You, who in evil days gone by
Proved the friend to all the people here.   190
How many a person is alive
Because your father in the past
Snatched him out of raging fever,
When he checked the plague at last.
You entered every stricken house,
Though at that time a young man still;
Many a corpse was carried forth,
Yet you came through and were not ill,
Surviving trial and hardship to the end;
The friend was aided by the Heavenly Friend.   200

ALL THE PEASANTS

May good health bless the worthy man,
Long may he serve as best he can!

FAUST

Bow down to Him whose teachings tell
Us how to serve, and who sends help as well.

(*He walks on with* WAGNER.)

WAGNER

What feelings, O noble man, must rise in you
Before the veneration of this crowd!
Oh, happy the man who gains such honors through
The gifts with which he is endowed!
The father shows you to his son,
Each hurries, questions everyone,   210
The fiddler stops, the dancers wait:
They form in rows, you pass in state,
While caps are waved and flung up high;
But little more and they would kneel
As if the Host were carried by.

FAUST

Only a few steps more, up to that stone—
Here, after our rambling, let us rest at last.
Here, lost in thought, often I sat alone,
Torturing myself with prayer and fast.
So rich in hope, so firm in faith was I,   220
With pleading hands, with tear and sigh,
The end of that dread plague I sought
From the Lord of Heaven to extort.
The crowd's applause now sounds like scorn to me.
Oh, could you read my inmost soul, you'd see
How little can the son or father claim
Such exaltation and such fame!
My father was a somber man of honor,
Who, with whimsical efforts, day by day
(Yet honestly enough in his own way),   230
Brooded on Nature and her holy sphere.
As did other adepts, he withdrew
And locked himself in his sooty cell to brew
A liquid to make the opposites cohere
By means of endless formulas he knew.
Two substances—a White Lily and a Lion Red—*
Were in tepid water mystically wed,
And, driven by an open burst of flame,
From one bridal chamber to another came.
If then the young queen shone within the glass   240
In brightly varied colors, one could tell
This was the remedy! Patients died, alas,
But no one raised the question: Who grew well?
So we, with hellish nostrums, spread more ills
Throughout these valleys and these hills,
Causing far more damage than the pest.

---

* In this jargon of the alchemists, elaborated by Goethe, the red lion
stands for mercuric oxide, the white lily for hydrochloric acid. Their
"offspring," a bright-colored precipitate, is the "young queen."

Poison to thousands I myself did give;
They withered away—yet I must live
To hear the barefaced murderers blest.

WAGNER

How can you yield to such despair? 250
Has not a good man done his share
By practicing with conscientious mind
The art entrusted to him by mankind?
If you revere your father as a youth,
You'll learn from him with eager will;
In manhood, if you further science, truth,
Your son may reach a goal far higher still.

FAUST

Oh, happy the man who hopefully aspires
Out of this sea of error to arise!
What man knows not, is just what he requires; 260
What man knows, he cannot use in any wise.
But let us not by gloomy spirits mar
This hour radiantly serene!
Behold! in the glow of sunset, from afar
The little houses shimmer, set in green.
The sun moves on and fades, the day is spent,
It hurries on to further fruitful birth.
Ah, that no pinions lift me from the earth
To follow close and closer its ascent!
Bathed in the eternal evening glow, 270
I would see the world beneath me, stilled;
The cliffs ablaze, the vales with quiet filled,
The Silberbach into golden streams would flow.
Not even the mountain gorge in wild display
Would then impede my godlike flight;
And soon the sea, each warmly sheltered bay,
Would lie before my wondering sight.

When it would seem the sun must sink at length,
A new urge fills me with new strength.
I speed on to drink the sun's eternal light,   280
Before me the day, behind me the night,
Heaven above, below the ocean swings;
A lovely dream while softly fades the sun!
Alas, not easily to the spirit's wings
Are bodily wings companioned. Yet each one
Is born with an innate desire
Which drives us up and forward to aspire,
As the lark above, unseen in cerulean skies,
Warbles its trilling melody while it flies,
As o'er the craggy, pine-clad height   290
The eagle, outstretched, poises in its flight,
And over sea and marsh the crane
Homeward gravitates again.

WAGNER

I too have often felt peculiar things,
Though never the pulsing drive to which you yield.
One wearies soon of forest and field,
And I shall never envy the bird its wings.
How different it is when spiritual joys assuage
Us, turning from book to book, page to page!
Then winter nights a blessing and charm unfold.   300
In holiness our beings glow,
And ah, if a precious parchment is unrolled,
The very heavens descend to us below.

FAUST

One instinct only are you conscious of,
Oh, never learn to know its counterstate!
Alas! two souls within my breast abide,
And each from the other strives to separate;
The one in love and healthy lust,

The world with clutching tentacles holds fast;
The other soars with power above this dust   310
Into the domain of our ancestral past.
Oh, if there be spirits here,
Between the earth and heavens holding sway,
Descend now from the golden atmosphere,
Lead me to new and varied life away!
Yes, were a magic mantle only mine,
Away to distant lands I'd lightly wing;
I would not change it for raiment however fine,
Not even for the mantle of a king!

WAGNER

Do not call upon that well-known swarm   320
Which permeates the vapory air;
From every corner they prepare
To injure men and do them harm.
From north with sharpened spirit-fangs they fly,
Pressing you with arrow-pointed tongues;
From east they move upon you hard and dry,
Nourishing themselves upon your lungs;
Sent from south, when desert whirlwind drives,
They scorch your head with glowing firebrands;
The west leads on a host which first revives,   330
Then drowns you with the fields and pasture lands.
They listen gladly, injure with fond intent,
Gladly obey, to cheat they gladly try;
From Heaven feigning to be sent,
They steal the tongues of angels when they lie.
But let us leave! Twilight shadows fall,
The air grows chill . . . mist covers all.
One learns to prize one's home at night.
Why do you stand and stare . . . What is the trouble?
What so attracts you in the failing light?   340

FAUST

D'you see that black dog, winding in and out the rye and
    stubble?

WAGNER

Long ago! Not much to that—far as I can tell.

FAUST

What d'you take the beast to be? Observe it well!

WAGNER

Why, for a dog who, as dogs do, runs about,
To sniff his master's footsteps out!

FAUST

Watch how in wide concentric rings
Near and nearer to us he springs!
If I'm not wrong, a streak of fire gleams
Directly in his wake.

WAGNER

I see a plain black dog—or so it seems;   350
The rest could be an optical mistake.

FAUST

He's drawing a magic coil—it seems to *me*—
For future bondage round our feet.

WAGNER

                          I see
He jumps about us, confused and filled with fear
At finding, not his master, but strangers here.

FAUST

The ring grows smaller . . . he is almost near!

WAGNER

There now, it is no phantom, but a dog!
It crawls upon its belly, snarls in play,
Wagging its tail in the usual doglike way.   360

FAUST

Come here to us! Come, do!

WAGNER

The creature really is absurd.
If you stand still, he'll wait for you,
He'll leap upon you at a word;
If something's lost, he'll fetch it quick,
Or jump into the water for a stick.

FAUST

You're right! There is no trace that one can call
A spirit's; just a well-trained dog, that's all.

WAGNER

Even a sage will be inclined
To love a dog well trained to mind.   370
He emulates your students, is so clever,
That he deserves to win your favor.

(*They pass through the gate of the city.*)

III

THE STUDY

FAUST *entering with the dog.*

FAUST

Now behind me meadowland and field
Are by the depths of night concealed;

With awe and with foreboding might,
Our better self asserts its right.
Now turbulent desires sleep, and free
From passions' stress and strain,
The love of man revives in me,
The love of God is stirred again.

Be quiet, dog! Don't race about that way!
Why do you sniff the threshold as you play?   10
Lie down behind the stove. If you do,
I'll give my choicest cushion up to you.
Since outside, on the hilly thoroughfare,
You pleased us, capering with zest,
I promise now to take you in my care
As a welcome, but a silent guest.

    Ah, when within our narrow cell
    The lamp once more throws out its friendly cheer,
    Then in our inmost being all is clear,
    And in the heart, which knows itself full well,   20
    Reason begins once more to speak,
    And hope begins to bloom again;
    The stream of life we yearn to seek,
    Ah, to the source of life could we attain!

Stop snarling, dog! Your noise is out of key
With sounds that sacredly
My very soul embrace!
Full well we know the human race
Scorns what it does not understand;
And grumbles at the good and beautiful   30
Which it finds difficult to command.
Will the dog, as men do, snarl and growl?

But, ah! although my will is of the best,
Contentment flows no longer from my breast.

Why must the stream so soon be dried,
Leaving me to thirst once more?
I've felt this longing oft before,
Therefore I know this want can be supplied.
To prize the supernatural we learn,
For revelation's light we yearn,   40
Which nowhere shines in worthier light
Than here in our New Testament. Tonight
I feel impelled to turn to the earliest text
And, with honest feeling, render next
The sacred original we teach
Into my belovèd German speech.

(He opens a volume and begins.)

"In the beginning was the Word!" so runs the text.
I'm balked already! On whom can I rely
For help? I cannot rate the Word so high,
And must translate it otherwise. I am perplexed!   50
If by the Spirit truly inspired, I ought
To translate thus: "In the beginning was the Thought!"
Do not let your pen race on ahead;
Dwell upon this opening line instead.
If it be Thought which in all things stirs to create,
Then "In the beginning was the Power," the text must state.
Yet even as I start to write this too,
Something warns me that it will not do.
The Spirit aids me! Suddenly I grasp the fact
And confidently write: "In the beginning was the Act!"   60

If we are to share this cell,
Dog, stop growling,
Stop that howling!
For I cannot stand, I fear,
Such a noisy comrade near.
One of us must say farewell
To this pleasant, quiet cell.

A truce to hospitality,
The door is open, you are free!
But whatever do I see?   70
Can this be natural? Can it be
A shadow? a reality?
How large my dog has grown—how tall,
Rising in power, fierce and strong!
That's not a canine form at all!
What specter have I brought along?
Almost a hippopotamus in size,
With gaping jaws and blazing eyes.
Oh, indeed! Well, I know *you!*
For all of your half-hellish crew   80
The key of Solomon will do!

SPIRITS (*in the corridor*)

Someone is trapped and caught within!
Stay out, let no one follow him!
Like a fox in a snare
The Hell-Lynx quakes there.
But give heed, give heed!
Hover to and fro,
Above, below,
He will soon be freed.
If aid ye can find,   90
Leave him not confined!
Many a good turn he's done
To everyone!

FAUST

First, to face the mighty beast,
I need the spell of the Four at least:

Glow, Salamander,
Undine, meander,
Sylph, disappear,
Gnome, labor here.

He who does not discern
The Four Elements, learn
Their secret force—
And properties, of course—
Can never be lord
Of the spirit-horde.

Salamander, at thy name
Vanish into flame!
Rushing waters unite,
O Undine!
Glow like a meteor bright,
O Sylph!
Bring aid to the house, and at my call,
Incubus! Incubus!
Come forth—end it all!

These Four at least
Are not hid in that beast.
It lies quite still and grins at me,
I have not hurt it yet, I see.
Hear me at length
Exorcise with more strength.

Fellow, art thou
A fugitive from Hell?
Behold the Sign!
This can compel
Dark hosts to incline.

With bristling hair it starts to swell!

Abject creature, take heed!
Canst thou not read
The sign of the Uncreated,
Whose name cannot be stated,
Who pervades the heavens far and wide,
The Being wantonly crucified?

Behind the stove it's relegated,
Like an elephant inflated,
Into vapor swiftly stealing,
Filling up the room complete.
Do not rise up to the ceiling!
Down now, at your master's feet!
You'll find my threat is not in vain,
I'll scorch you with a holy flame!   140
Do not wait to know
The thrice dazzling glow!
Do not wait to know
My strongest arts and strongest powers!

(MEPHISTOPHELES, *garbed as a traveling scholar, steps for-*
ward from behind the stove as the mist disappears.)

MEPHISTOPHELES

Why all this noise, sir? What can I do for you?

FAUST

So *that* was hidden in the brute! My word!
A traveling scholar? It's too absurd!

MEPHISTOPHELES

Good evening, learned sir! I do declare
You have made me sweat for fair.

FAUST

What's your name?   150

MEPHISTOPHELES

                A trifling question; furthermore,
From one who utterly spurns the Word,
And, scoffing at appearance, would explore
The depths of being to its core.

FAUST

With gentlemen like you one can discern
The nature, if the name we learn;
Thus one knows well what it implies
To call you Destroyer, Liar, God of Flies.
Who, then, are you?

MEPHISTOPHELES

Part of that power which operates 160
Ever in evil, yet good ever creates.

FAUST

Tell me what this riddle of yours implies!

MEPHISTOPHELES

I am the Spirit that denies!
And justly so; for all that's born
Deserves to be destroyed in scorn.
Therefore 'twere best if nothing were created!
Destruction, sin, wickedness—plainly stated,
All which you as evil classified—
That is my element, there I abide!

FAUST

You call yourself a part, yet as a whole appear to me? 170

MEPHISTOPHELES

I am telling you the simple facts.
Though man, the foolish microcosm, acts
As if complete he thought himself to be.
I am part of that part which was the Absolute,
A part of that Darkness which gave birth to Light,
The arrogant Light which would dispute
The ancient sway of Mother-Night,

To claim her space, and yet the struggle dies;
Light to corporeal substance cleaves with force;
From it flowing, this substance it beautifies,   180
Yet corporeal substance checks it on its course.
And so I hope it won't be long before,
With substance it will perish evermore.

FAUST

Now I grasp your worthy scheme!
Your plans for universal ruin fail,
So you begin upon a smaller scale.

MEPHISTOPHELES

I've not accomplished much, I'll frankly state!
This power which against nothingness is hurled,
This something—this your clumsy world—
Though constantly I've tried to injure it   190
By earthquake, tempest, or volcanic flame,
Has not been really touched one bit!
Unharmed, the sea and land remain the same,
While man and beast, that cursed earthy stuff—
What I have managed there is little enough.
What endless numbers have I not wiped out!
Yet new blood ever circulates about.
So it goes on! It drives me frantic! Everywhere
The earth, the water, and the air,
In dryness, wetness, warmth and cold,   200
A thousand vital germs unfold.
Until, if I had not reserved the flame,
I should have nothing as my own to claim.

FAUST

Against the healing, creative force which you resist—
Eternally opposed, with might and main—
You thrust your cold, malignant Devil's fist,

Spitefully clenched, yet clenched in vain.
You singular Son of Chaos, I should say
A different task had best be sought!

MEPHISTOPHELES

We'll give this matter further thought,   210
And talk about it more another day.
Might I withdraw this time? Will you allow . . .

FAUST

I don't see why you ask me that,
I've just begun to know you now.
Come whenever you wish to chat:
Here's the window, there the doors,
And the chimney is also yours.

MEPHISTOPHELES

I'll own up! I cannot leave at will.
A trifling hindrance forces me to stay:
That wizard-foot upon your sill . . .   220

FAUST

What! The pentagram* is in your way?
Well, well! Tell me then, you Son of Hell,
How did you enter since you cannot leave?
A spirit of your sort, how could one deceive?

MEPHISTOPHELES

Look carefully! It's not drawn well;
The outer angle—nearest me—
Is slightly open, as you see.

---

* A five-pointed star, here the same as the "wizard foot," a magic symbol used to keep witches out of the house.

FAUST

What a piece of luck! It's *you*,
And now my prisoner! . . . Yes,
By merest chance, a great success!   230

MEPHISTOPHELES

The dog, on leaping in, saw nothing new,
But things are different now—I perceive
The Devil is caught and cannot leave.

FAUST

Why not slip out that window frame?

MEPHISTOPHELES

Devils and phantoms on this law agree:
Where they steal in, they must slip out again.
Slaves of the second law, of the first we're free.

FAUST

So even Hell has its own laws? Why, then
Would it not be possible to make
A binding compact with you gentlemen?   240

MEPHISTOPHELES

We'll carry out the tasks we undertake;
You shall enjoy all that we promise you.
As this cannot be swiftly brought about,
Let us discuss it next time too.
For this time spare me—let me out!

FAUST

Only a moment more—do stay;
First tell me some good tidings.

MEPHISTOPHELES

No!
Set me free! I'll soon return; then you may
Ask me what you please—I do not care.   250

FAUST

You let yourself into the snare,
I did not set a trap for you tonight.
He who catches the Devil should hold him tight;
A second time he will not catch him there.

MEPHISTOPHELES

At your pleasure, I'm prepared to stay
And keep you company awhile,
Provided that my arts (and quite your style)
May profitably pass your time away.

FAUST

I'll watch you willingly indeed;
Let your arts be pleasing and proceed!   260

MEPHISTOPHELES

My friend, in this one hour, freed,
Your senses will experience more
Than in all your humdrum years before.
The music gentle spirits sing;
The lovely images they bring
Are not mere magic-phantasy.
First your sense of smell will be invoked,
Next your palate be provoked.
Then feelings glow ecstatically!
We need not plan out any part;   270
We are assembled! Come now, start!

THE SPIRITS (*singing*)

Vanish, ye gloomy
Arches on high.
Gaze on us,
Lovely and friendly
Blue sky!
Oh, would the murky
Clouds disappear!
Tiny stars, sparkle,
Soft sunbeams,   280
Shine here.
Children of Heaven,
Spirits of love,
Bowing and trembling,
Hover above.
Undying longing
Next we behold;
Soft flowing draperies,
Wind and unfold,
Covering the bowers,   290
Covering the field,
Where for life, deep in reverie,
True lovers yield.
Bower on bower,
Tendrils entwine!
Clustering grapes,
Heaping in vats,
Are squeezed in the press,
Leaping in streams,
Into bubbling wine steams   300
And ripples o'er stones,
Lovely and bright;
Then leaving behind
The glittering height
It spreads into lakes

Of purest delight
To feed the green hills.
Thence in swift flight,
Drinking pure bliss,
The feathery race   310
Flies in clear space
Direct to the sun;
Flies to the isles
Which on the sea
Seem to be floating
Gracefully free;
Where chorus on chorus
Shouting with glee
Over the meadows
Dancing we see.   320
In the clear air
Seeking their play,
Spirits are climbing
The hills far away;
Others are swimming
Over the sea,
Others soar free,
All toward life,
All to the far,
Loveliest star!   330

MEPHISTOPHELES

He sleeps! Ye delicate aerial youths, 'twill do!
Ye have sung him sound asleep!
For this concert I'm in debt to you.
No, Faust, you are not yet the man to keep
The Devil fast! Dreams of beauty flutter free,
Plunge him into seas of phantasy!
But to break the threshold's magic spell,
A rat's sharp tooth is needed. I can tell

I shall not conjure long; right near
A rat goes scurrying by and soon will hear.   340

    The Lord of rats and Lord of mice,
    Of frogs and flies, of bugs and lice,
    Commands that you at once appear
    To gnaw that bit of threshold clear,
    On which a drop of oil is cast:
    Here you come hopping, hopping fast!
    To work! The point which keeps me bound
    Is on the outer angle found.
    Another bite, that frees the door!
    Now, Faust, dream on! until we meet once more.   350

FAUST (*awaking*)

Have I been deceived again today?
Did a bevy of spirits, vanishing, make it seem
The Devil appeared to me in a lying dream,
And that a black dog ran away?

IV

THE STUDY

FAUST   MEPHISTOPHELES

FAUST

Who's knocking? Come in! Who's annoying me again?

MEPHISTOPHELES

It's I.

FAUST

Come in!

MEPHISTOPHELES

It must be said three times quite plain.

FAUST

Then come in!

MEPHISTOPHELES

Hm! That tone pleases me!
I only hope we shall agree!
To rid you of your moods, I appear
This time dressed as a cavalier.
With coat of scarlet, trimmed with gold,   10
A stiff little silken cape, a bold
Cock feather in my cap, in pride
A rapier dangling at my side;
And once for all I roundly advise
That you adopt this dress likewise,
So that with no restraint, set free,
You'll know what life can really be!

FAUST

I'd feel, no matter what be my attire,
The pain of life, lived in a humdrum way.
I am too young to be without desire,   20
Too old, too old merely to play.
What has the world to offer me?
Thou must renounce! Renounce! That song
Is one which rings eternally
In our ears the whole life long,
And during life, throughout its course,
Each hour sings till it is hoarse.

In horror only, I waken with the sun
And bitter tears could weep, to see
The day whose course will not fulfill   30
One single wish of mine—not one—
But thwarts each budding joy that's sent,
By carping self-disparagement;
Through twisted views it keeps suppressed
The creative stir within my breast.
Even at night I'm forced, it seems,
To lie and worry on my bed,
But there I find no rest; instead
I'm terrified by wildest dreams.
The god who dwells within my breast   40
Can rouse my inner self at will,
Commanding my energies, and still
He cannot change my outer fate.
And thus existence is a burden—
Death I long for, life I hate!

MEPHISTOPHELES

Yet death is never a wholly welcome guest.

FAUST

Oh, fortunate the man in victory blest
Whose brow with blood-stained wreath is bound,
Whom death, after a frenzied dance, has found
Clasped against a woman's breast!   50
Oh, had I only expired in that hour
Of rapture, exalted by the Spirit's power!

MEPHISTOPHELES

Yet someone did not drink one night
A certain brownish liquid . . . Well, did he?

FAUST

Spying, it seems, is your delight!

MEPHISTOPHELES

I am not all-knowing, yet much is known to me.

FAUST

When from that dreadful conflict drawn away
By sounds of sweet familiar harmony,
Fragments of childlike feeling, lingering in me,
Betrayed me with echoes of a happier day.   6c
Now I curse all that seeks to cheat
The soul with luring phantasy,
Binding it with flattery and deceit
Into this pit of misery!
Cursed before all that lofty thought
In which the spirit itself doth shroud!
Cursed be the dazzling forms which sought
Upon our senses to press and crowd!
Cursed be all dissembling dreams
Of fame and everlasting life!   70
Cursed be the flattery of what we own,
As vassal, plough, as child and wife!
Cursed be Mammon when with treasure
He spurs us on to daring deeds,
While merely for our idle pleasure
Spreading the cushions for our needs!
Cursed be the soothing juice of the grape!
Cursed be love's ecstatic call!
Cursed be hope! Cursed be faith!
And cursed be patience most of all!   80

CHORUS OF SPIRITS (*invisible*)

Woe! Woe!
Thou hast laid low
The beautiful world
By the force of thy blow!
It totters, it crashes!

A demigod smashes!
We carry the fragments
Into the void,
To bemoan and deplore
The beauty destroyed.   90
Earth-born
Thou hast both power and might!
Create it anew
More glowingly bright;
In thy breast let it spring!
A new life commence
With clarified sense,
This thou must do,
Then new songs will ring.

MEPHISTOPHELES

These are my tiniest minions who   100
With ancient wisdom
Would counsel you
To enter the world
Of deed and desire.
Hark! Flee this lonely state
Where the senses and life-force
Seek to stagnate!

Cease to play with your affliction then,
Which like a vulture feeds upon your life;
The worst of company would make you feel   110
That you are still a man amongst men.
Yet I don't mean to thrust you back
Into the common pack.
I am not of the very great,
Yet if you'll take me as a mate
And go your way through life with me,
I will willingly agree
To be yours on the spot and be

Your very comrade to the grave
And if I suit—
I'll be your servant, be your slave.

120

FAUST

And in return what must I do for you?

MEPHISTOPHELES

You have a long time ere that note is due.

FAUST

No, no! The Devil is an egoist,
And does not casually assist
Another person—merely for love of God!
State all conditions plain and clear:
A servant such as you brings danger near.

MEPHISTOPHELES

Here I'll pledge myself at your command
To serve implicitly and without rest;
If, when in the *beyond* we stand,
You'll do the same for me at my request.

130

FAUST

The *beyond* fills me with small concern;
If you dash this world to fragments first,
The other may arise in turn.
Out of this earthly source my happiness springs,
And *this* sun shines upon my sufferings.
From both conditions could I separate,
Then let what will, and can, appear!
Further, I do not care to hear
If in a future one feels love or hate,
Or if in any other sphere
There is a higher or a lower state.

140

MEPHISTOPHELES

On these terms you may well say yes.
Commit yourself; in days to come I mean
To show you all the arts which I possess;
I'll give you what no mortal yet has seen.

FAUST

What, poor Devil, could you give at best?
Was ever human spirit, in its striving,
Understood by such a breast?   150
Yet have you food which never satisfies—
Red gold that like quicksilver flies,
Melting in the outstretched palms,
A game at which one never wins,
A girl who even in my arms
Upon a neighbor casts her eyes,
The honor of a godlike aim
Vanishing like a meteor's flame?
Show me fruits which rot ere gathered from the tree,
And trees which daily bloom anew!   160

MEPHISTOPHELES

Demands like these do not embarrass me,
Such treasure I can offer you.
But there will come a time, my friend,
When you'll desire to feast in peace instead.

FAUST

If ever I stretch upon an idler's bed,
Then let my doom descend!
If ever through lying flattery
You lure me into self-complacency,
If ever through pleasure you succeed
In tricking me into feeling satisfied,   170
Let *that* day be my last!
This is my wager!

MEPHISTOPHELES

Done!

FAUST

Agreed!
If ever to the moment I should say
"Oh, stay! Thou art so fair!"
Clap me into fetters then and there,
Then to destruction I shall gladly go!
Then may the death bells toll,
Then from your service you are freed at last;   180
The clock may stop, the hands may fall,
My time will be forever past!

MEPHISTOPHELES

Consider well! I shall remember all.

FAUST

You have the fullest right thereto;
This compact was not entered wantonly.
I'm a menial if I persist in what I do,
Yours or whose—what difference can there be?

MEPHISTOPHELES

Today then, as your servant, I will start
And at your table carry out my part.
But one thing more: a few brief words to show,   190
In the event of life or death!

FAUST

And so,
You pedant, you ask for something in writing? Absurd!
Have you never known man—nor his word?
Is it not enough that I must be
Bound by my spoken word eternally?

Does not the world, by all the streams of life compelled,
Rush on, and by a promise am I held?
Still this delusion lurks within each heart,
And who from this deceit desires to part?   200
Happy the man in whose heart truth is revealed;
He will not rue a sacrifice he makes!
Yet any piece of parchment, written and sealed,
Is a specter from which mankind shrinks and quakes.
The word is dead before it leaves the pen,
But wax and leather dominate all men.
Spirit of Evil, what do you wish from me?
Brass, marble, parchment, paper—which shall I use?
Shall I write with chisel or quill? Come, choose!
Or perhaps a stylus? Your choice is free!   210

MEPHISTOPHELES

Why must you suddenly declaim
In this exaggerated style?
Any bit of paper will do! Meanwhile,
With just a drop of blood, inscribe your name.

FAUST

If you are satisfied by such an act,
Let the farce continue to the end.

MEPHISTOPHELES

Blood is a most peculiar fluid, friend!

FAUST

Have no fear that I shall break the pact!
The trend and aim of all my energy
Will be to carry out my vow. Alas!   220
I thought myself superior, and I see
My proper place lies in your class.

The mighty Spirit cast me off in scorn,
And Nature closed her portals in distrust.
The thread of thinking has been torn,
All knowledge fills me with disgust.
Let us in depths of sensual delight
The force of violent passions quell.
By an impenetrable magic spell
Let miracles arise in sight! 230
Into the whirl of time we'll press,
The hurry-scurry of events! In full measure
Let pain and pleasure,
Worry and success,
Alternate as best they can;
Restless activity proves the man.

MEPHISTOPHELES

There is no goal prescribed, however high.
Nibble at everything you please.
Snatch at opportunity as you go by,
Whatever gives you joy, I hope agrees; 240
Only don't be bashful, just fall to.

FAUST

But, once for all—pleasure is not the question.
To poignant joy and frenzy I would yield,
To quickening joy, enamored hate;
Nor shall my heart, from thirst of knowledge healed,
Henceforth to any sorrow bar the gate.
Deep in my self I will enjoy and find
The fate which is the lot of humankind;
Within my soul I'll grasp the worst and best,
Heaping their griefs, their joys upon my breast; 250
Thus my own self to their selves I'll extend,
To be destroyed, as they are, in the end.

MEPHISTOPHELES

Oh, believe me, who for many a thousand year
Have chewed this hard and wretched fare,
No one from the cradle to the bier
Digests this bitter leaven anywhere!
Believe one of us, this entire parade
Only for a God was made!
He dwells in radiance forever bright,
Us he thrust in darkness out of sight,   260
As for *you*—be satisfied with day and night.

FAUST

Despite you, I'm determined!

MEPHISTOPHELES

                                    A capital thought!
Still, one thing seems a trifle wrong:
Time is short, and Art is long.
It struck me—if perhaps you could be taught—
With a poet to associate.
Let him give his thoughts free sway
And heap upon your worthy pate
The noblest traits he can display: 270
The lion's force,
The stag's swift pace,
The passion of the Italian race—
With northern constancy, of course.
Let him discover the secret way to link
Nobility with guile and think
Up a clever, well-constructed plan,
To make you love wisely, yet with youthful flame.
I'd like to meet this very man,
"Sir Microcosm"* would be his name.   280

---

* That is, he would be in himself a small universe, an epitome of life.

FAUST

What am I then, if I can never gain
The crown of humanity which from afar
Every sense is striving to attain?

MEPHISTOPHELES

You are, at the end, just what you are!
Get yourself a wig with curls a score,
Get yourself stilts a yard high or more,
You are, at the end, just what you are!

FAUST

I feel that I have struggled to attain
The riches of the human spirit, in vain;
If now at last I sit me down to rest, 290
No fresh vitality surges in my breast;
In height I'm not a hair's breadth more,
No whit nearer the Infinite than before!

MEPHISTOPHELES

My good fellow, you perceive this fact
Correctly in the ordinary light;
More cleverly we now must act,
Before the joys of life elude us quite.
The deuce! Of course your hands and feet,
Head and backside are yours complete!
All I enjoy spontaneously— 300
Does that the less belong to me?
If for six stallions I can pay,
Are not their forces mine? And may
I not speed on, as fresh and fine
As if four and twenty legs were mine?
Let all this brooding be! Up then,
Off with me into the world of men!

I tell you, a fellow who speculates
Is like a beast on a barren strand,
Led by an evil spirit round and round,   310
While all about lies fair green pasture land.

FAUST

How shall we start?

MEPHISTOPHELES

We'll leave with speed.
What is this—a martyr's cell?
What kind of life is this to lead,
Boring yourself, the youngsters as well?
Leave that to your colleague, the ancient vat!
Why do you bother threshing straw? At that,
The best which you could ever learn
You dare not tell these lads in turn!   320
There, I hear one in the hall!

FAUST

I cannot see him now at all.

MEPHISTOPHELES

Poor fellow, he had so long a wait,
He must not leave disconsolate.
Hand me your cap and gown! I see
This costume will look rich on me!

(*He disguises himself in* FAUST's *cap and gown.*)

Leave it to me as I proceed!
Fifteen minutes is all I need;
While you for a pleasant flight prepare with speed.

(*Exit* FAUST)

MEPHISTOPHELES (*in* FAUST's *long robe*)

Scorn reason and science if you can,   330
The highest powers yet bestowed on man!
Through illusion and with magic arts
Let the lying spirit strengthen its hold,
Then, body and soul, I'll pin you down at last!
Fate gave to him a spirit wildly bold
Which drives him faster and still more fast,
And with untrammeled impulse sweeps him past
Earthly joys which he might hold!
I'll drag him through the wildest life,
Through meaningless inanity;   340
He'll wriggle, struggle, stuck fast in his plight;
Because of his insatiate appetite,
Food and drink shall dangle in sight,
Before his greedy lips quite plain,
Yet he shall cry for sustenance in vain.
Had he not given himself to the devil today,
He would have perished anyway!

(*A* STUDENT *enters.*)

THE STUDENT

I came a little while ago,
And, filled with deference, come here
A man like you to meet and know   350
Whom all men honor and revere.

MEPHISTOPHELES

You please me by your courtesy!
A man like other men you see.
Perhaps you have enrolled somewhere?

THE STUDENT

Do take me into your care!
I've come with courage—with rather bold
High spirits, and not too little gold;
My mother scarce would let me go;
Yet something worth while I'd like to know.

MEPHISTOPHELES

You have found out the proper place.   360

THE STUDENT

Quite frankly, I should like to quit:
These walls, these halls, like endless space,
Do not attract me, I'll admit.
It's all so cramped wherever one goes—
No trees or green—no, not one bit!
While classrooms, with their chairs in rows,
Make me lose hearing, sight, and wit.

MEPHISTOPHELES

You'll grow accustomed none the less!
No child will take its mother's breast
At the start with willingness,   370
Yet soon it feeds with utmost zest.
Thus to wisdom's breast held tight,
You'll crave your nurture more each day.

THE STUDENT

I'll clasp her neck with genuine delight,
If you will point me out the way.

MEPHISTOPHELES

Ere you proceed, tell me if you can
What course of study you have found.

THE STUDENT

I long to·be a learned man,
Possessing knowledge deep and sound
Of heaven, and the earth as well;
Of nature and of science too.

MEPHISTOPHELES

You're on the right track, I can tell;
Let no distraction hinder you.

THE STUDENT

With heart and soul I have begun;
Yet speaking frankly, if I may,
I'd like some freedom and some fun
Upon a summer holiday.

MEPHISTOPHELES

Use well your time, for all too soon it flies!
System will teach you to save time. My friend,
This is the first step I advise,
Follow a course of Logic to the end.
Your spirit will be drilled to think,
Cramped as if in Spanish boots; so taught,
It then will circumspectly slink
Along the path of stodgy thought,
And cannot zigzag to and fro
As a will-o'-the-wisp is wont to go.
Days will be spent in teaching you
That all you once did easily,
Like eating, and like drinking too,
Now's done by rule of one, two, three!
Frankly, to manufacture thought
Is like a masterpiece by a weaver wrought!
A thousand threads one treadle guides,
To and fro the shuttle slides,

380

390

400

Subtly the unseen threads unite,
Till one move knits a thousand tight.
Up steps your philosopher to the fore
Proving it *must* be so; what's more,
The first was so, the second so,   410
Therefore the third and fourth are so;
If the first and second were not so,
The third and fourth would not be so.
While scholars laud this—don't forget
Not one was ever a weaver yet.
Who would study and describe the living rightly,
Seeks first to drive the spirit forth and thinks
That in his hands he clasps the pieces tightly,
But missing, alas! are the spiritual links.
*Encheiresin naturae,** is chemistry's cry,   420
Mocking itself, not knowing why.

THE STUDENT

I don't quite understand you, sir.

MEPHISTOPHELES

Next time it will come easier,
When you have learned how everything should be
Reduced and classified most properly.

THE STUDENT

I feel confused by what you've said,
As if a mill wheel whirled inside my head.

MEPHISTOPHELES

Above all else next you must turn
To Metaphysics; manage to learn
Its content thoroughly and attain   430
What never was meant for human brain.

---

* "Nature's method"—an allusion to certain arguments about chemi-
cal combination in the textbook of one of Goethe's teachers.

For what you can or cannot understand,
An excellent word is right at hand.
Be sure that during this half-year
To punctuality you adhere.
You'll have five hours when you start;
At the bell be in your seat
Prepared beforehand to repeat
All your paragraphs by heart,
So you observe the teacher quotes   440
Only what the book has stated;
Yet be as zealous taking notes
As though the Holy Ghost dictated!

THE STUDENT

No need to say that twice! I quite
Agree how helpful this will be;
What one has down in black and white,
One can take home contentedly.

MEPHISTOPHELES

Select the faculty which appeals to you.

THE STUDENT

For Jurisprudence I feel no call.

MEPHISTOPHELES

I do not blame you there at all,   450
I know this calling through and through.
Law and Justice eternally descend,
Direful as a disease which has no end;
They drag themselves from race to race,
Cautiously moving from place to place.
Reason becomes nonsense, benevolence a pest,
And woe to you, heir to this bequest!
Yet of the law which is our inborn right,
Alas, that question never comes to light.

THE STUDENT

You make my own distaste more strong.   460
Oh, lucky the man you help along!
Come to think of it, I'd like Theology.

MEPHISTOPHELES

I'd hate to see you led astray by me.
Where'er this science is concerned,
From false paths it is hard to keep;
In it such hidden poisons sleep,
From Medicine it's scarce to be discerned.
Here again, one man had best be heard:
Swear fast by your professor's word.
In general to words stick fast!   470
Then, into the temple of certainty,
Through safe, sure gates you'll pass at last.

THE STUDENT

Yet words must harbor some ideas.

MEPHISTOPHELES

Of course! Only don't worry yourself; you'll find
Precisely where the meaning slips your mind
A word at proper time appears.
With words 'tis easy to dispute,
For words build systems to the dot,
To words all faith one can impute,
From words no one can steal a jot.   480

THE STUDENT

My questions have detained you, sir,
Still, I must bother you once more.
Will you not say a trenchant word
On Medicine and its deep lore?
Three years is such a little time,

And heavens! the field is far too wide.
One could much sooner find the way
Had one a sign-post for a guide.

MEPHISTOPHELES (*aside*)

I'm sick of this pedantic vein!
I've got to play the Devil again.   490

(*Aloud*)

The spirit of Medicine can be grasped with ease;
Study the great and little world, my friend,
To let it all go in the end
As God may please!
Why ramble about in science uselessly?
Each man learns only what he can.
But he who snatches opportunity
Proves himself the real man!
You have a rather fine physique,
And are not shy; you'll find it true,   500
That when you learn self-confidence
Others will have faith in you.
Learn to manage women! You will see
The endless *Oh*'s and *Ah*'s which they
Complain of everlastingly
Can all be cured in just one way:
And if you are halfway discreet
You'll have them eating from your hands.
They will be led by your degree
To think your art all arts commands;   510
As an opening, the various spots caress
Which others strove to reach for years,
And her little pulse in rhythm press;
Then, with a fiery sidelong glance,
Clasp her round the slender waist
To see how tightly she is laced.

THE STUDENT

That's more like it! The where and how one sees!

MEPHISTOPHELES

Gray, my dear friend, are all theories,
And green the golden tree of life.

THE STUDENT

It all seems like a lovely dream, I swear!   520
May I intrude again? And might I dare
To tap your wisdom at the source?

MEPHISTOPHELES

I'll do all I can for you, of course.

THE STUDENT

I cannot tear myself away
Without requesting you to sign
My book of autographs. Please, just a line!

MEPHISTOPHELES

With pleasure!

>   (*He writes and returns it to the* STUDENT.)

THE STUDENT (*reading*)

*Eritis sicut Deus, scientes bonum et malum.**

>   (*He closes the book reverently and withdraws.*)

MEPHISTOPHELES

Follow my relative the snake and the ancient text;   529
Of your likeness to God you will grow weary and vexed!

---

* "Ye shall be as gods, knowing both good and evil"—the serpent's
promise in Genesis.

(FAUST *enters.*)

FAUST

Where shall we go?

MEPHISTOPHELES

Why, where you please.
We'll see the small world, then the great;
With profit and delightful ease
You'll fool away time in this new state!

FAUST

Yet with this flowing beard of mine,
I lack the social ease I need.
This attempt will not succeed,
In company I cannot shine;
People make me feel so small;   540
I'll never be at ease at all.

MEPHISTOPHELES

Once gain self-confidence, all that will end;
Then you will know how to live, my friend.

FAUST

How do you intend to leave?
Where are your servants, coach and pair?

MEPHISTOPHELES

We've but to spread my mantle out,
And it will bear us through the air.
However, on this daring flight
Take only luggage that is light.
Some heated gas which I have found   550
Will lift us quickly from the ground.

If we're light, we'll quickly rise from here;
Congratulations on your new career.

V

AUERBACH'S CELLAR IN LEIPZIG

A carousal of jolly comrades

FROSCH

Will no one drink, no one laugh?
I'll teach you to make faces at me! Today
You are all like damp, limp chaff—
Usually you blaze away.

BRANDER

That's your fault; we get nothing from you,
No nonsense, no dirty jokes—what's one to do?

FROSCH (*pouring a glass of wine on his head*)

There you have both!

BRANDER

Double-damned swine!

FROSCH

You wanted a joke—well, take mine!

SIEBEL

Who picks a scrap goes out that door;   10
At the top of your lungs, chorus, guzzle and roar!
Up! Hallo! Ho!

ALTMAYER

I'm done for! Come here!
Bring cotton-wool! The fellow split my ear.

SIEBEL

Only when the arches echo and ring
Do we feel how powerfully the basses sing!

FROSCH

Right! And out with him who takes offense!
A tara-diddle-diddle!

ALTMAYER

A tara-diddle-dee!

FROSCH

Our throats are tuned, so let's commence!   20

(*He sings.*)

The Holy Roman Empire,
How the hell does it hang together?

BRANDER

A horrid song! Shame! A political song,
A rotten song! Thank God that you
With the Roman Empire have naught to do!
At least I think it a capital thing
That I'm neither chancellor nor king.
But since a leader we must select,
Come then, a Pope let us elect.
You know the qualities which seem   30
To raise a man in our esteem.

FROSCH (*singing*)

Soar up, soar up, Dame Nightingale,
My love with a thousand greetings hail!

SIEBEL

No greetings to your love! That I won't allow!

FROSCH

Yes, greetings and kisses! You can't stop me anyhow!

(*He sings.*)

Lift the latch! The night is still.
Lift the latch! The lover wakes.
Shut the latch! For morning breaks.

SIEBEL

Sing on, sing on, and praise her as you will!
I'll have the laugh on you before you're through.   40
She made a fool of me—she'll do the same to you.
May a goblin-lover be her fate!
He'd dally with her at the crossroads all right!
An old goat, clumping home from the Blocksberg* late,
Prancing, dancing, and bleating good night!
I tell you a fellow of real flesh and blood,
For that young hussy is much too good!
I'll send no greetings to that lass,
Save with a stone to smash her window glass!

BRANDER (*pounding on the table*)

Attention! Attention! All listen to me!   50
Sirs, you'll admit that I know how to live;
Some love-sick people are here, so I see

---

* The same as the Brocken, where witches and devils, often in the
form of animals, gather on Walpurgis Night. See Scene XXI below.

A jolly good-night song we must give;
They have the right to expect that from me!
Attention! The latest song out! Up now, sing
A rousing chorus, with vigor and swing!

(*He sings.*)

In a cellar nest once lived a rat,
Whose paunch grew ever smoother,
For all he ate was butter and fat,
Till he looked like Dr. Luther.   60
One night the cook set poison 'round;
And then the world grew as hot, he found,
As though loving were burning his carcass!

CHORUS (*shouting*)

As though loving were burning his carcass!

BRANDER

He ran around, he ran about,
Swilling up each puddle;
He gnawed and scratched the house throughout,
Naught helped him out of the muddle.
He writhed and whirled, his pain was such,
The poor thing soon was suffering as much   70
As though love were burning his carcass!

CHORUS

As though loving were burning his carcass!

BRANDER

By anguish propelled into open day
He ran to the kitchen scuffling,
Fell on the hearth and squeaking lay,
With pitiable sniffling and snuffling,
The poisoner laughed with murderous glee:

"Ha, ha! He's piping his last!" said she,
As though love were burning his carcass!

CHORUS

As though loving were burning his carcass!   80

SIEBEL

How these dull sophomores love this stuff!
I think it is a pretty sell
To give these poor rats poisoned stuff.

BRANDER

You seem to like rats rather well?

ALTMAYER

That bald pot-belly, fat and sleek!
Disaster makes him tame and meek;
In the swollen rodent he can see
His portrait, lifelike as can be.

FAUST   MEPHISTOPHELES

MEPHISTOPHELES

First I wanted to bring you here
Into a jolly atmosphere,   90
To see how lightly life can slip away.
To these people each day is a holiday;
With little sense and plenty of ease,
They spin about in circling trails,
Like kittens chasing after their tails.
As long as headaches they appease,
And hosts give credit everywhere,
They live content and free from care.

BRANDER

From their curious bearing they appear
To be on a journey; it is clear   100
They've not been here an hour tonight.

FROSCH

A toast to Leipzig! By Jove, you're right!
Leipzig, the little Paris, gives tone to its people!

SIEBEL

What d'you take them for?

FROSCH

                        Leave it to me!
I'll get them drinking, then, no doubt,
I'll ferret their secrets as easily
As one can draw a child's tooth out.
They're of the nobility, that I can tell,
They look proud and discontented as well.   110

BRANDER

I'll bet they're fakers, on a spree!

ALTMAYER

Perhaps.

FROSCH

        I'll trip them up—watch me!

MEPHISTOPHELES (*to* FAUST)

Though he has them by the collar, it is clear
Such people can't sense when the Devil is near

FAUST

Good day to you, gentlemen!

SIEBEL

Thanks and the same.

(*In a low voice, looking at* MEPHISTOPHELES *from the side*)

He drags one foot; is the fellow lame?

MEPHISTOPHELES

Will you permit us to sit with you?
Your company will cheer us up in lieu   120
Of decent wine, which we can't get here.

ALTMAYER

Quite a fastidious person, I fear!

FROSCH

Perhaps from Rippach* you started late?
Was it dark when you supped with Sir Hans today?

MEPHISTOPHELES

Today we traveled by and did not wait.
Last time we talked at length; he'd much to say
About his cousins, and, when he had done,
He sent his kind regards to everyone.

(*He makes a bow to* FROSCH.)

ALTMAYER (*aside*)

You got it there! He's on, I bet!

SIEBEL

He's a sly dog!   130

---

* A village near Leipzig of which the name suggests "the sticks,"
just as Sir Hans suggests the country bumpkin.

FROSCH

Wait! I'll get him yet.

MEPHISTOPHELES

Unless I'm wrong, did we not hear
A very well trained chorus singing?
Song must sound very fine and clear,
Back from these vaulted arches ringing!

FROSCH

Perhaps you're a virtuoso? Am I wrong?

MEPHISTOPHELES

Oh, no! The power is weak, though desire is strong.

ALTMAYER

Give us a song!

MEPHISTOPHELES

Any number, and very fine.

SIEBEL

Be sure they're of a brand-new strain!　　　140

MEPHISTOPHELES

We have just returned from Spain,
The lovely land of music and of wine.

(*He sings*)

　　Once upon a time there was a king
　　Who had a large pet flea—

FROSCH

Listen! Did you get that, fellows? A large pet flea!
Quite a neat little guest, it seems to me.

MEPHISTOPHELES (*singing*)

Once upon a time there was a king
Who had a large pet flea
On whom he lavished everything,
As if a son were he.   150
He called his tailor; at his behest,
The tailor promptly flew:
"Here, measure the lad for coat and vest,
And measure him for breeches, too!"

BRANDER

Don't fail to warn the tailor ere he ceases,
He must take measurements to a hair!
For if he values his head, I swear
The breeches must fit without any creases!

MEPHISTOPHELES

In finest silk and velvet,
He was completely dressed,   160
With ribbons on his jacket,
And a cross upon his breast.
Prime minister was his station,
A splendid star had he,
While at court each flea relation
Became a lord of high degree.

The courtiers and court ladies
Were very badly smitten;
The queen and her attendants
Were stung and sorely bitten;   170
Yet nobody dared to flick 'em off,
When he itched at night;
But we will flick and nick 'em off,
As soon as we feel 'em bite!

CHORUS (*shouting*)

Yes, we will flick and nick 'em off,
As soon as we feel 'em bite!

FROSCH

Bravo! Bravo! That was fine!

SIEBEL

May this be the end of every flea!

BRANDER

Nick 'em off with your finger cleverly!

ALTMAYER

Hurrah for freedom! Hurrah for wine!   180

MEPHISTOPHELES

In freedom's honor I'd take a glass
Gladly, were your wine of a better class.

SIEBEL

We don't want *that* from you again!

MEPHISTOPHELES

Did I not fear the landlord would complain,
I would treat every worthy guest
To some of our cellar's very best.

SIEBEL

Just bring it on—I'll take the blame!

FROSCH

We'll praise you if the wine is good—make haste!
But don't hand out too stingy a taste;
For if the judge's role be mine,   190
I've got to have a good guzzle of wine.

ALTMAYER (*aside*)

As I suspected, they're from the Rhine.

MEPHISTOPHELES

Get me a gimlet.

BRANDER

Why, what for?
Your casks are not outside the door?

ALTMAYER

The host has a toolbox right behind.

MEPHISTOPHELES (*takes the gimlet; to* FROSCH)

What's to your taste? Make up your mind!

FROSCH

How's that? Have you some of every kind?

MEPHISTOPHELES

Each to his taste. The choice is free.

ALTMAYER (*to* FROSCH)

Already you're licking your chops, I see!   200

FROSCH

If I am to take my choice of wine,
Let it be German, and from the Rhine.

(MEPHISTOPHELES *bores a hole in the edge of the table at
the place where* FROSCH *is sitting.*)

MEPHISTOPHELES

Fetch me a little wax for stoppers, quick!

ALTMAYER

Hm—that's just a juggler's trick.

MEPHISTOPHELES (*to* BRANDER)

And you, sir?

BRANDER

Oh, champagne for me,
And highly sparkling let it be!

(MEPHISTOPHELES *bores; meanwhile one of the others has
made the wax stoppers and plugged the holes.*)

At times one can't abstain from foreign stuff,
As what is good is often hard to get;
A German does not like a Frenchman, yet   210
He drinks his wines down willingly enough.

SIEBEL (*as* MEPHISTOPHELES *approaches where he is sitting*)

I must confess I hate sour wine,
Give me a glass from a really sweet case!

MEPHISTOPHELES (*boring*)

Tokay shall flow at once from the vine.

ALTMAYER

No, sirs, look me straight in the face!
You're making fun of us, I know you are.

MEPHISTOPHELES

With such distinguished guests? Oh, *no!*
That would be going a bit too far.
Only speak out! Hurry up though!
With what sort of wine can I serve you?   220

ALTMAYER

What's the difference? Any kind will do.

(*After the holes have all been bored and plugged*)

MEPHISTOPHELES (*making curious gestures*)

> Mellow grapes the vine stem bears!
> Crooked horns the old ram wears;
> Wine is juicy, of wood the vine,
> The wooden table too gives wine.
> Into the depths of Nature peer!
> Have faith, a miracle is here!

Draw the plugs and drink your fill!

ALL (*together, as they draw out the stoppers and each fills his glass with the wine he has chosen*)

O lovely fountain, rising at our will!

MEPHISTOPHELES

Be careful, lest a drop should spill.   230

(*They drink repeatedly.*)

ALL (*singing together*)

> We feel as hoggishly well, do we,
> As five hundred cannibals off on a spree!

MEPHISTOPHELES

How well they feel—see, the rabble is free!

FAUST

I should like to be leaving right away.

MEPHISTOPHELES

Pay attention! Bestiality
Will now reveal itself in striking display.

SIEBEL (*drinks carelessly—the wine spills upon the ground and turns to flame*)

Help! Fire! Help! Hell-fire is sent!

MEPHISTOPHELES (*addressing the flame*)

Be quiet, friendly element!

(*To the young men*)

This time 'twas a taste of hell-fire merely!

SIEBEL

What's this? Just wait! You'll pay dearly,   240
You don't know whom you're dealing with really!

FROSCH

Don't you try that trick a second time!

ALTMAYER

I think we'd better quietly send him packing.

SIEBEL

Well, sir? Is common sense so lacking
You try this hocus-pocus pantomime?

MEPHISTOPHELES

Keep still, old vat!

SIEBEL

So you insult us—damned broomstick!

BRANDER

Just wait! You'll get it fast and thick.

ALTMAYER (*pulls a stopper out of the table—fire flies in his face*)

I'm burning—I'm burning!

SIEBEL

Witchcraft! Strike!   250
The fellow's an outlaw! Hit as you like!

(*They draw their knives and rush at* MEPHISTOPHELES.)

MEPHISTOPHELES (*with solemn gestures*)

False words and images though fair,
Change thoughts and scenery everywhere!
Be here—be there!

(*They stand amazed and look at one another.*)

ALTMAYER

Where am I? What a lovely land!

FROSCH

Vineyards! Do I see clearly?

SIEBEL

And grapes at hand!

BRANDER

Beneath these arbors of different shapes,
See, what vines! See, what grapes!

(*He takes* SIEBEL *by the nose. The others do the same, one to another, and raise their knives.*)

MEPHISTOPHELES (*as above*)

Error, from their eyes loose the band!   260
Mark you how the Devil turns a jest!

(*He disappears with* FAUST; *the young men separate.*)

SIEBEL

What's happened?

ALTMAYER

What?

FROSCH

Was that your nose?

BRANDER (*to* SIEBEL)

How . . . is this yours in my hand!

ALTMAYER

It was a bolt that went through every limb!
Get me a chair—my head begins to swim!

FROSCH

But, first, do tell me what took place!

SIEBEL

Where has he gone? If I can trace
That fellow, he'll not escape alive!   270

ALTMAYER

I saw him . . . there,

Going out the cellar door! I swear,
He was riding a wine cask! . . .
Oh, but my feet are heavy as lead!

(Turning toward the table)

What if the wines were flowing ahead!

SIEBEL

It was an illusion—a cheating show.

FROSCH

Yet I drank real wine—or it seemed to me so.

BRANDER

What about the grapes? Were they false, too?

ALTMAYER

Who says miracles don't come true!

VI

THE WITCH'S KITCHEN

A large cauldron stands over the fire upon a low hearth. In the steam that rises out of the cauldron various forms appear. An APE *sits beside the cauldron and skims it, watching that it does not boil over. The* HE-APE, *with the* YOUNG ONES, *sits near by and warms himself. The ceiling and walls are covered with curious paraphernalia of witchcraft.*

FAUST   MEPHISTOPHELES

FAUST

This frenzied, senseless witchcraft sickens me!
Do you really promise I shall be

Completely cured by all this frantic mess?
From such a crone am I to seek assistance?
And will her filthy slops remove no less
Than thirty years from my existence?
Pity me, if you know no better thing!
Already hope is vanishing.
Cannot Nature or a noble spirit find
A healing balsam of any kind? 10

MEPHISTOPHELES

You're talking sense again, my friend! Now look!
There is a natural way of growing young,
But that is written in another book;
The chapter is a curious one.

FAUST

I must know it!

MEPHISTOPHELES

       Good! This process does not need
Magic, gold, or medicine:
Go to the fields and there begin
Straightway to hoe and dig with speed,
Keep your mind and self restrained 20
Within a narrow, humble sphere,
And by the simplest nurture be sustained;
Live with cattle as cattle live, nor think it ill
To fertilize yourself the land you till.
This is the best way, it is plain,
At eighty to grow young again!

FAUST

I am not used to that! I do not feel
That I could ever stoop to use a spade.
A narrow sphere of life has no appeal!

MEPHISTOPHELES

Then we must call in the witch to aid.   30

FAUST

But why just this old hag? I don't see
Why you can't brew the drink yourself for me!

MEPHISTOPHELES

A pretty pastime! Why, I'd make
A thousand bridges in the time 'twould take.
For more than art and science enter here,
This work requires patience too.
A tranquil spirit labors many a year,
Yet time alone makes potent this strange brew.
And precious things alone we choose
As ingredients to use.   40
The Devil taught her how, 'tis true enough;
And yet the Devil cannot make the stuff.

(*Gazing at the* ANIMALS)

See what a charming breed is here displayed!
This is the man! That is the maid!

(*To the* ANIMALS)

It seems your mistress is out today?

THE ANIMALS

Out of the chimney she flew away,
Out of the house
Off to a carouse!

MEPHISTOPHELES

How long does her carousing require?

THE ANIMALS

Until we have warmed our paws at the fire. 50

MEPHISTOPHELES (*to* FAUST)

What do you think of this dainty pet?

FAUST

More absurd than anything I've seen yet!

MEPHISTOPHELES

Really, a conversation of this kind
Is most appealing to my mind.

(*To the* ANIMALS)

Abominable creatures, come, speak out!
What sort of pap are you stirring and stewing?

THE ANIMALS

A mess of thin soup for beggars we're brewing.

MEPHISTOPHELES

You have many a customer, no doubt.

THE HE-APE (*approaching and fawning on* MEPHISTOPHELES)

O the dice swiftly throw,
Rich let me grow, 60
Let me rake in my gains!
The world is unfair,
If I'd gold, I declare,
I'd also have brains.

MEPHISTOPHELES

Oh, how lucky the ape would feel,
If he had a turn at a roulette wheel!

(*Meanwhile the* YOUNG APES *have been playing with a large ball which they now roll forward.*)

THE HE-APE

The world is a ball:
See it rise and fall,
And roll and spin;
It rings like glass,   70
But soon breaks, alas!
It's hollow within.
Here bright it gleams,
There brighter seems,
Alive am I!
Dear son, I say,
Do keep away,
For you must die!
'Tis made of clay,
In pieces 'twill fly.   80

MEPHISTOPHELES

What do you do with the sieve?

(*The* HE-APE *takes it down.*)

THE HE-APE

If you came here to thieve,
I'd know you right away.

(*He runs to the* SHE-APE *and lets her look through it.*)

Look through the sieve!
Do you know the thief,
Dare you name him today?

MEPHISTOPHELES (*drawing near the fire*)

What of this pot?

THE ANIMALS

The simple sot!
Does not know the pot,
Does not know the kettle! 90

MEPHISTOPHELES

Surly beast!

THE HE-APE

Bring that feather duster at least
And sit on the settle!

(*He motions to* MEPHISTOPHELES *to sit down.*)

FAUST (*who has been standing before a mirror all this time, now drawing near, and then drawing away*)

What heavenly vision . . . what do I see
Within the magic mirror plain!
O Love, lend me your swiftest wings,
Bear me to her domain!
Ah, if I stay not rooted to this place,
If I but dare to venture near,
Then as through a mist the imaged face 100
Of the fairest woman is made clear!
Can woman really be as fair?
Do I on this recumbent body gaze
As on a heavenly epitome?
Can this be found on earth?

MEPHISTOPHELES

Naturally
If a god torments himself six days,
And in the end cries "Bravo" in self-praise,
Something clever must occur!

For this time look your fill, be satisfied!   110
I'll pick you up a darling just like her,
And fortunate the happy man
Who as a bridegroom leads her home in pride!

(FAUST *continues to gaze into the mirror.* MEPHISTOPHELES,
*stretching himself out upon the settle and playing with the
feather duster, continues to speak.*)

Here I sit like a king on a throne,
The scepter I hold, I lack the crown alone.

THE ANIMALS (*who have been making all sorts of curious
gestures, bring a crown to* MEPHISTOPHELES *with much
chatter*)

Oh, be so kind,
With blood and sweat
The crown to bind!

(*They handle the crown awkwardly, and it breaks into
two pieces around which they hop.*)

'Tis done this time!
We speak and see,   120
Yet listen and rhyme!

FAUST (*still before the mirror*)

I'll go quite mad! O pity me!

MEPHISTOPHELES (*pointing to the* ANIMALS)

Even my head begins to shake!

THE ANIMALS

If luck is ours,
To stir our powers,
Thoughts we'll make!

FAUST (*as above*)

Oh, my heart begins to burn!
Let's be off, away from here!

MEPHISTOPHELES (*in the same attitude*)

One must say this much in return:
They are true poets and sincere!   130

(*The cauldron, which the* SHE-APE *has neglected to watch until now, begins to boil over. There is a burst of flame which blazes up the chimney. With a horrible shriek the* WITCH *comes flying down through the flames.*)

THE WITCH

Ow! Ow! Ow!
Damnable beast! Accursed sow!
Neglects the kettle, burns her dame!
Accursed beast!

(*Perceiving* FAUST *and* MEPHISTOPHELES)

What doth appear?
Why are you here?
Who are you anyhow?
What do you want now?
May torturing flame
Burn the marrow of your frame!   140

(*She plunges the ladle into the cauldron and sprinkles flames over* FAUST, MEPHISTOPHELES, *and the* ANIMALS. *The* ANIMALS *whimper.*)

MEPHISTOPHELES (*reversing the feather duster, which he holds in his hand, and smashing about amongst the glasses and pots*)

Crack! Crash!
There lies the trash!
There lies the glass!
It's just a bit of tomfoolery,
Keeping time, you ass!
To your melody.

(*As the* WITCH *starts back, full of horror and anger*)

You know me then? You hag! Abomination!
You recognize your master and your lord?
What hinders me from thrashing you,
From smashing you, and your monkey horde!   150
Have you no more respect for the crimson coat than that?
Don't you know the long cock feather in my hat?
Have I in any way concealed my face?
Must I even announce my presence in this place?

THE WITCH

Forgive my greeting so uncouth!
And yet I see no cloven hoof;
Besides, your ravens—where are they?

MEPHISTOPHELES

This time you may get off this way;
It is a long time, I'll admit,
Since last we met, and I can tell   160
That culture coating all the world so well
Has even tinged the Devil a bit.
The Northern Phantom* is outmoded—where
Do you see either claws or tail or horn?
While, as regards the foot which I can't spare,
That would harm me socially; and I've worn

---

* An allusion to the Enlightenment's war against superstition: belief in a literal devil no longer exists, though devilishness still does—
as the lines that follow reaffirm.

Padded calves for many a year
Like many another young man here.

THE WITCH (*dancing about*)

Reason and sense I wholly lack,
Since my Lord Satan has come back! 170

MEPHISTOPHELES

Woman, I forbid that name!

THE WITCH

Why so?
How it has harmed you, I'd like to know.

MEPHISTOPHELES

That name became a legend long ago,
Yet men are none the better, it's quite plain;
Freed from the Evil One, evil ones remain!
Call me simply Baron, we'll call it square;
I'm a cavalier like any other cavalier,
And lest you doubt my noble blood—look here!
This is the coat of arms I bear! 180

(*He makes an indecent gesture.*)

THE WITCH (*laughing immoderately*)

Ha! Ha! That's just what you prefer!
A shameless rogue, as you always were!

MEPHISTOPHELES (*to* FAUST)

My friend, note what I do and say;
Learn to handle witches the proper way.

THE WITCH

Now tell me, sirs, what do you desire?

MEPHISTOPHELES

Some of your famous juice; but I require
The oldest stuff; for, as you see,
Time redoubles its potency.

THE WITCH

With pleasure! Here I have a flask
From which I sometimes sip a drink;   190
And which, moreover, does not stink;
I'll gladly pour you what you ask.

(*Aside*)

Yet if he drinks it unprepared, you know,
He cannot live more than an hour or so.

MEPHISTOPHELES

He is a good friend, he will stand it well;
I don't begrudge your cellar's best to him.
Draw your circle, speak your spell,
Fill up a goblet to the brim!

(*The* WITCH *describes a circle with fantastic gestures and
places strange things in it; meanwhile the glasses begin to
ring, the cauldron booms and makes music. Finally she
brings out an enormous book and stands the* APES *in the
center of the circle, to serve her as a reading desk and
hold the torches. She beckons to* FAUST *to approach.*)

FAUST (*to* MEPHISTOPHELES)

Tell me what this is leading to. I've had enough!
These crazy gestures, this idiotic stuff,   200
All this vulgar trickery—
I know and hate it thoroughly.

MEPHISTOPHELES

Fiddlesticks! Laugh at it if you can;
Don't be such a serious man!
She uses hocus-pocus as doctors do,
So that the potion may agree with you.

(*He makes* FAUST *enter the circle.*)

THE WITCH (*with great emphasis begins to recite from the book*)

This you must know!
Make ten out of one,
Then let two go,
Make an even three, 210
Then rich you will be.
Discard the four!
Of five and six,
Says the witch, you'll fix
Up seven and eight,
Till it comes out straight:
And nine is one,
And ten is none,
This is the witch's one-times-one.

FAUST

The hag's delirious, far as I can tell! 220

MEPHISTOPHELES

There's more to come, I know it well,
It jingles on and on, page after page;
I've wasted so much time on it in vain,
For perfect contradictions will remain
Mysteries to a fool as to a sage.
The art is new yet old as it can be,

And has been used for ages past:
With three and one and one and three,
Error instead of Truth is cast.
They teach and jabber undisturbed;   230
Who cares to bother with a fool?
Man usually believes, if he but hears a word,
That it contains a meaning, as a rule.

THE WITCH (*continues*)

The lofty might
Of scientific light
Is hidden everywhere!
He who pays no heed
Receives it, indeed,
Without any trouble or care!

FAUST

What silly nonsense the creature drools!   240
My head is splitting in two. Good Lord,
I feel as if I listened to a horde
Of a hundred thousand chattering fools!

MEPHISTOPHELES

Enough, O worthy Sibyl! Enough!
Bring on your drink, and pour the stuff
Quickly into the goblet, to the brim.
My friend is safe, your drink won't injure him.
He's a man of high degrees, of great renown,
Who in his day sipped many a good drink down.

(*The* WITCH, *with many ceremonies, pours the liquid into a goblet; as* FAUST *lifts it to his lips, a little flame leaps up.*)

MEPHISTOPHELES

Down with it promptly! Don't be slow!   250
It will do your heart good right away.
What! Hand-in-glove with the Devil you go,

Yet shrink from fire in dismay?

(*The* WITCH *breaks the circle.* FAUST *steps out.*)

Now out with you—step quickly, please!

THE WITCH

I hope the taste you had agrees.

MEPHISTOPHELES

If I can do you a favor, why, you might,
Remind me of it on Walpurgis Night.*

THE WITCH

Here is a song for you to sing!
Its effect on you will be astonishing.

MEPHISTOPHELES

Come quickly, let yourself be led about;   260
A proper perspiration must commence
So that the poison's strength flows in, then out.
Later I'll teach you to prize a noble indolence,
And soon with sense of pleasure you will know
How Cupid stirs and races to and fro.

FAUST

Let me look into the mirror—just once more!
That form was so fair I saw in it before.

MEPHISTOPHELES

No! No! The paragon of womankind,
Alive and real, you'll shortly find.

(*Aside*)

With this drink in your body you soon will see   270
Helena in every woman instantly.

---

* See note on page 82.

VII

A STREET

Faust   Margarete

MARGARETE *passes by*

FAUST

My pretty lady, may I offer you
My arm to see you home?

MARGARETE

I'm not a lady, I'm not pretty,
I can go home quite well alone.

(*She frees herself and goes away.*)

FAUST

What a lovely girl went there!
I've never seen one like her anywhere.
Such modesty, such sweetness—yet
Something pert in what she said.
In all my life I won't forget
Those cheeks so flushed, those lips so red.   10
The way she shyly dropped her eyes,
Is deeply stamped upon my heart.
How short and sharp were her replies,
That was the most delightful part!

(MEPHISTOPHELES *enters.*)

See here, get me that girl at once!

MEPHISTOPHELES

Why—

Which one?

FAUST

The one who just went by.

MEPHISTOPHELES

That one? She just left the priest,
Who purged her from all sin—by talk at least!   20
I sneaked in right behind her chair.
She is an innocent for fair,
And goes to the confessional for naught;
I have no power over her sort.

FAUST

But surely she is past fourteen!

MEPHISTOPHELES

You're talking like a libertine,
Who craves each blossom that he sees,
Thinking all charm and virtue may
Be plucked by him with utmost ease.
It does not always work that way!   30

FAUST

My worthy Master Moralist,
From preaching law and common sense, desist.
I tell you briefly and outright:
Unless that lovely little thing
Is lying in my arms tonight—
At midnight you and I will part.

MEPHISTOPHELES

Consider the practical side: indeed
Fourteen days at least I need
In order to ferret out a way.

FAUST

Had I but seven hours in all   40
I really should not need to call
The Devil to lead that naïve thing astray.

MEPHISTOPHELES

You're talking like a Frenchman now!
Please do not fret! And anyhow,
What's the use of rushing pleasure?
Your joy is never half so great
As when you dillydally at leisure
And, with all sorts of nonsense, wait
To pet and mold the moppet well,
As many foreign stories tell.   50

FAUST

I've appetite enough without that fuss.

MEPHISTOPHELES

No scolding or nonsense—I'm serious.
I tell you, that lovely child who just went past
Never can be won by going fast,
Or taken by storm; we must depend
On skill and strategy to this end.

FAUST

Fetch me something the angel wears!
Take me to her place of rest!
Fetch me her garter as a token,
Fetch me the kerchief from her breast!   60

MEPHISTOPHELES

That you may see how I, in your pain,
Try to serve with might and main,
I'll waste no time, but right away
I'll bring you to her room today.

FAUST

Shall I see her—have her?

MEPHISTOPHELES

No!
She will be at a neighbor's when we go;
Meanwhile, left alone an hour or so,
You can imbibe her atmosphere and dwell
Upon the hopes of future joys as well.   70

FAUST

Can we go now?

MEPHISTOPHELES

No, it's still too soon.

FAUST

Get me a gift for her this afternoon.

                                                    (*Exit.*)

MEPHISTOPHELES

Gifts already? Bravo! He'll win, I'm bound!
I know of many a lovely grove,
And many an ancient treasure trove;
I must be off and scout around.

                                                    (*Exit.*)

VIII

EVENING

A small, neatly kept room. MARGARETE *braiding and tying up her hair.*

MARGARETE

I'd give anything if I knew
Who that gentleman was today!
He looked so gallant, so handsome too!
He's a titled person anyway,
That much I could plainly see—
Else he would not have been so bold with me!

(Exit.)

(MEPHISTOPHELES *enters with* FAUST.)

MEPHISTOPHELES

Come in—quietly—but come in!

FAUST *(after a moment's silence)*

I beg of you—leave me alone!

MEPHISTOPHELES *(peering about the room)*

Not every girl would be so neat.

(Exit.)

FAUST

Welcome, dusky twilight, thou who dost shed   10
Upon this hallowed place thy gentle light!
Grip fast my heart, love's torturing delight,
Which on the dew of hope is fed.

Here peace and order breathe about me,
Here deep contentment weaves a spell.
What abundance in this poverty!
What blessing in this little cell!

(*He throws himself into a leather armchair which stands
beside the little bed.*)

Oh, take me also, who with open arms received
The joys and sorrows of a world gone by!
How often gathered round th'ancestral chair,   20
Groups of children drew anigh!
Perhaps, too, my little love came here,
With rounded childish cheeks; here she would stand
And, grateful for the Christ child's gift,
Reverently kiss her grandsire's wrinkled hand.
I feel your spirit of order, O beloved girl!
Which about me seems to play,
Teaching you mother-wise, from day to day,
To smooth the tablecloth you lay,
To keep the sand so fresh beneath your feet.   30
O little hand, so godlike and so sweet!
Through you this cottage becomes a veritable heaven.
And here!

(*He lifts one of the curtains of the bed.*)

     A tremor of delight seizes me!
Here many an hour I'd linger in reverie!
O Nature, you shaped as in a gentle dream
An innate angel into form. . . . Here lay
The child whose soft breasts pulsed
With rising life . . . here the design
Was woven with holy purity   40
Into a semblance of the divine.

And you! What led you here? What are you doing?

Why is your heart so heavy and so sore?
Why do you feel so deeply moved?
Miserable Faust! I know you no more!

Am I surrounded by an atmosphere of magic?
Urged on by sheer enjoyment, now I find
I am being dissolved in a dream of love!
Are we the sport of every gust of wind?

What if she were this moment to come in,   50
How atone your insolent wantonness!
You jackanapes! How small you'd be,
Prone before her, languishing in distress.

MEPHISTOPHELES (*entering*)

Make haste! I see her coming.

FAUST

Away! Away! Never will I return.

MEPHISTOPHELES

Here's a little casket, weighing quite a bit;
From its hiding place I've carried it.
Put it in the wardrobe—anywhere—
That's going to turn her head, I'll swear!
Inside I let some trifles lie,   60
Fine enough to catch another by,
For a child's a child and play is play.

FAUST

I wonder . . . should I?

MEPHISTOPHELES

                    Why question and delay?
You don't intend to keep the gems, do you?
May I suggest that, if you do,

You cease this lustful longing, and so spare
Me further trouble, further care.
I really hope you are not stingy!
I wring my hands and scratch my head—   70

(*He places the casket in the wardrobe and turns the key
in the lock again.*)

Quick, let's be off!—
To help you mold that sweet young thing
After your heart and will; instead,
You stand stock-still and stare and stare
As if you were entering the lecture hall,
As if before you in the flesh
Physics and Metaphysics were standing there!
Come, let's go!   (*Exeunt.*)

MARGARETE (*entering with a lamp*)

It seems so close, so sultry now,

(*Opening a window*)

And yet it's not so warm today.   80
It makes me feel, I just can't say—
But I wish mother were at home somehow.
From head to foot I'm shuddering—
Oh, I *am* a foolish, timid thing!

(*She begins to sing while she undresses.*)

There was a king of Thule
True unto the grave,
To whom his dying mistress
A golden goblet gave.

It was to him most precious,
He cherished it for years;   90
And at each feast he drained it,
His eyes then moist with tears.

When death was close upon him,
He counted towns and land,
Then ceded all his riches
Save the goblet in his hand.

Surrounded by his vassals,
At the royal board sat he,
In a vast ancestral chamber,
In the castle by the sea.   100

Up rose the hoary reveler,
Drained his last life-glow,
Then flung the sacred goblet
Into the tide below.

He watched it swaying, filling,
And sinking 'neath the sea.
Then, his eyelids closing,
Ah, never more drank he!

(*She opens the wardrobe to arrange her dresses and sees
the little jewel casket.*)

How did that pretty casket get in here?
I'm sure I locked the wardrobe door—that's queer!   110
My, it's handsome! I wonder what's inside?
Someone brought it here to pawn, maybe,
And mother lent some money on it. Why—
There, on the ribbon hangs a little key!
I'd love to open it. . . . I think I'll try!
What's this? God in Heaven! Look,
I've never seen such things before!
A set of jewels! Even a titled lady
Might wear these—on a holy day, what's more.
I wonder how the chain would look on me!   120
Who could ever own such jewelry?

(*She decks herself with the jewels and steps before the mirror.*)

If only just the earrings were my own!
One looks a different person right away.
What good are youth and beauty to you alone?
It is all very well and good,
Beyond it, there's not much to say;
Folk praise you—but half in pity, I am sure.
All strive for gold, and in the end
It seems as if on gold all things depend.
How hard it is to be poor!   130

IX

PROMENADE

FAUST, *lost in thought, walks up and down.*
Enter MEPHISTOPHELES.

MEPHISTOPHELES

By the pain of rejected love! By all the elements of Hell!
If I only knew something worse by which to swear!

FAUST

What's up? What ever stung you? Well, well, well!
What a face! I've never seen one like it anywhere.

MEPHISTOPHELES

I'd give myself to the Devil in a trice,
If I myself were not a devil in fact!

FAUST

It rather suits you to rave like a lunatic!
You seem to be off your head, from the way you act!

MEPHISTOPHELES

Imagine! The jewels I scraped up for Gretchen* today,
A sanctimonious priest has filched away!   10
Her mother looked them over and, it appears,
Began at once to quake with hidden fears.
That woman has the keenest sense of smell!
She snuffles over prayer books time and again,
Till sniffing at each object she can tell
Whether it be sacred or profane;
As for the jewels, she was soon aware
That very little blessing could be there.
"My child," she cried, "ill-gotten gain is sure
To waste the blood, and is for the soul a lure;   20
We'll offer these to Mary, through whose grace
We shall have heavenly manna in their place!"
But little Gretchen made a face and thought:
"What about the gift-horse? Why, it's clear
No wicked person ever could have brought
These jewels in this clever manner here."
Her mother called in the priest, he came with speed,
Gave the gems one look of crafty greed,
And, taking in quietly what he saw,
Held forth: "Now, that's a pious frame of mind!   30
Who conquers self wins grace, you'll always find.
The Church has such a healthy maw,
And though it's gobbled many a land and state,
As yet it never overate.
Dear faithful souls, alone the Church digests
Any ill-gotten treasure or bequests."

FAUST

Such is the universal game,
Jews and emperors do the same.

---

* Gretchen, once again, is the diminutive of Margarete.

MEPHISTOPHELES

He pocketed the bracelet, chain, and rings,
As if they were mere trashy things,   40
Thanking them, without any if's or but's,
As though he carried off a basket of nuts.
He promised them celestial gain—they sighed,
Were much impressed and edified.

FAUST

And Gretchen?

MEPHISTOPHELES

        Sits there restless, overwrought,
Not knowing what she should or ought to say.
She dreams about the jewels night and day,
Yet more about the donor than she ought.

FAUST

It grieves me that my darling has to fret.   50
Go, get her at once another set—
The first was not much anyway.

MEPHISTOPHELES

Of course to you it's all child's play!

FAUST

Now arrange matters as *I* think best.
Hang around her neighbor! For the rest—
Be no milksop or devil in a dither!
Fetch me a new set of jewels hither!

MEPHISTOPHELES

Certainly, sir, with all my heart, I'll run.

(*Exit* FAUST.)

That lovesick fool! He'd puff away
The galaxy of stars, the moon, the sun,   60
Just to give his sweetheart fun!

(*Exit.*)

X

NEIGHBOR'S HOUSE

MARTHE (*alone*)

May God forgive my dear old man,
He really did not treat me fair!
Off to foreign parts he ran,
And left me moping in despair.
I never worried him—not I!
God knows I loved him, and with all my might.

(*She weeps.*)

Perhaps he is dead— Oh, my! Oh, my!
If I could only have it black on white!

MARGARETE (*entering*)

Dame Marthe!

MARTHE

What is it, Gretchen dear?   10

MARGARETE

My knees are almost giving way!
I've found another box—look here,
It's ebony! 'Twas in my wardrobe today,
And things much grander. . . . See, a set
Handsomer than the one before.

MARTHE

Now don't you go telling your mother yet,
Or she'll whisk them off to church once more!

MARGARETE

Do see them! Oh, do look at them!

MARTHE (*putting the jewels on her*)

You *are* a lucky creature, sweet!

MARGARETE

Ah no, for I cannot be seen in them,   20
Neither in church, nor on the street.

MARTHE

Come over often here to visit me,
And wear the jewels secretly;
Parade before the mirror an hour or so,
And we'll enjoy ourselves. In time, you know,
There's sure to be a birthday, a pretext
To let the jewels be seen, just one by one—
At first the chain, the earrings next;
I'll think up something, should your mother suspect.

MARGARETE

Who could have brought both little boxes here?   30
There's something in it very queer.

(*A knock*)

Good Heavens—what if that be mother!

MARTHE (*peering through the blinds*)

It is a stranger. . . . Please come in.

(MEPHISTOPHELES *enters.*)

MEPHISTOPHELES

I made so free and came right in;
Ladies, excuse the liberty.

(*He steps back respectfully from* MARGARETE.)

'Tis Dame Marthe Schwerdtlein I want to see.

MARTHE

Here I am—what do you want with me?

MEPHISTOPHELES (*aside to her*)

I know you now, so that will do;
A distinguished visitor is with you.
Excuse me for having made so free;   40
I'll call this afternoon at three.

MARTHE (*aloud*)

Why, child, of all the funny things!
He takes you for a lady, dear.

MARGARETE

The gentleman is much too kind, I fear;
I'm just a poor young girl. The rings
And ornaments are not my own.

MEPHISTOPHELES

Ah, but it's not the jewelry alone;
She has an air about her, a charming way!
I am delighted I may stay.

MARTHE

What brought you here? I wish I knew . . .   50

MEPHISTOPHELES

If only my story ended happily!
I only hope you won't blame me.
Your husband is dead—and sends his greetings to you.

MARTHE

Is dead? That faithful soul! Oh, my!
My husband is dead! Oh, I shall die!

MARGARETE

Please bear up, dear Dame Marthe, do!

MEPHISTOPHELES

Hear the sorrowful story through!

MARGARETE

I hope that I shall never love;
Over a loss like this I'd grieve to death.

MEPHISTOPHELES

Joy has its sorrows as sorrow has its joys.   60

MARTHE

Tell me where he drew his dying breath!

MEPHISTOPHELES

He was buried in Padua close by
The church of St. Anthony; his bones now lie
In a cool eternal resting place,
A truly consecrated space.

MARTHE

Did you not bring me—well, a small bequest?

MEPHISTOPHELES

Oh, yes! A great and solemn request!
He wants three hundred masses: save this behest,
My pockets are completely bare!

MARTHE

What! No good luck piece? No trinket there   70
Which every workman stows in his sack with care,
As a keepsake till the very end,
And would starve or beg, sooner than spend!

MEPHISTOPHELES

It grieves me, madam, more than I can express.
But truly he did not waste his little store.
He repented deeply for his faults—yes,
Bewailing his bad luck still more.

MARGARETE

Ah, that men are so unfortunate!
Many a requiem I'll surely say!

MEPHISTOPHELES

You are a lovable, worthy child;   80
You deserve to marry right away.

MARGARETE

That is out of the question, though.

MEPHISTOPHELES

If not a husband, meantime, perhaps a beau.
Heaven could not offer greater charms
Than to hold a darling like you in one's arms.

MARGARETE

That is not the custom in this place.

MEPHISTOPHELES

Custom or not—it often is the case!

MARTHE

Please, sir, continue.

MEPHISTOPHELES

I stood by his side
At his deathbed, which was little more 90
Than a heap of rotted straw; yet a Christian he died,
Finding far greater debts charged to his score.
"How I despise myself," I heard him cry,
"Deserting my wife and trade to go to sea!
Ah, the memory is killing me,
Oh, could she forgive me ere I die!"

MARTHE (*weeping*)

Dear, good fellow! I forgave him long ago.

MEPHISTOPHELES

"And yet, God knows! She was more to blame than I."

MARTHE

There he lied! What! At the brink of the grave, to *lie!*

MEPHISTOPHELES

His mind was wandering at the end, no doubt, 100
If I am only halfway a judge. He said:
"There was no time for fun, nor could I loaf about;
Came children, then I had to earn their bread,
And all that is implied, with worry and care;
Yet not once could I sit down in peace to eat my share."

MARTHE

So he forgot my love and faith, as well
As all my drudgery both day and night!

MEPHISTOPHELES

Not at all, he thought of it with all his might!
"When we set sail from Malta," I heard him tell,
"I prayed for wife and children ardently,   110
And Heaven cast a favoring eye on me.
We took a Turkish merchantman whose hold
Was laden with the mighty Sultan's gold;
Then bravery its due reward obtained,
And, as was only just and fair, I gained
A liberally apportioned share."

MARTHE

How's that? Where?
Has he hidden it? How?

MEPHISTOPHELES

Who knows where the winds have carried it by now!
As he was wandering in Naples without a friend,   120
A pretty girl took him in tow;
Such love and faith did she bestow,
He felt the consequences till his end.

MARTHE

The wretch! To rob his children! Then, indeed,
All this misery and need
Could not change the shameful life he led.

MEPHISTOPHELES

But don't you see, that's why he's dead!
Now were I in your place here,
I'd wear my mourning modestly one year,
And meanwhile for a new beau look round.   130

MARTHE

S'help me, not easily in this world can be found
Another like my first! There scarce could be
A sweeter fool! . . . Ah, if only he
Had not been quite so fond of a roving life,
Of foreign wine, of foreign girls and vice—
And into the bargain the cursèd dice!

MEPHISTOPHELES

Come, come, things would have gone all right no doubt
If he had only really tried
To overlook as much as you did, on *his* side.
In the same situation, I swear 'tis true,   140
I'd exchange a ring myself with you.

MARTHE

Go on, sir, you're making fun of me!

MEPHISTOPHELES (*aside*)

I'd best be off before this gets absurd!
She'd hold the Devil to his word.

(*To* MARGARETE)

What about your heart? Is it free?

MARGARETE

Sir, what do you mean to imply?

MEPHISTOPHELES (*aside*)

You innocent child!

(*Aloud*)

Ladies, good-bye.

MARGARETE

Good-bye.

MARTHE

      Yet one thing more before you go: 150
I'd like to have some proof to show
He died, was buried—when, where, and how.
I've always been a stickler for propriety,
And should like a death notice in the papers now.

MEPHISTOPHELES

Yes, madam, by two witnesses, the truth
Is best confirmed. A clever youth
Is traveling with me whom I'll bring
To a notary to settle everything.
I'll go and fetch him.

MARTHE

      Oh, yes, please do!   160

MEPHISTOPHELES

Will this young lady be with you?
He's a fine young man, has traveled much,
Knows how to please the ladies, too.

MARGARETE

Oh, the gentleman would make me blush.

MEPHISTOPHELES

No king on earth would have the right!

MARTHE

In my garden, then, behind my house,
We will await you gentlemen tonight.

XI

A STREET

F<small>AUST</small>   M<small>EPHISTOPHELES</small>

FAUST

How are the plans? Advancing? Soon complete?

MEPHISTOPHELES

Bravo! I find you aflame? That's right!
Soon Gretchen will be yours; you'll meet
At neighbor Marthe's house tonight.
That woman was expressly made
To ply a pandering gypsy trade!

FAUST

Good!

MEPHISTOPHELES

    Something's asked of us as well.

FAUST

One good turn deserves another.

MEPHISTOPHELES

We've but to take a valid oath to tell   10
That her dead husband's limbs repose
At Padua in sacred ground.

FAUST

That's clever! First we'll go there, I suppose?

MEPHISTOPHELES

*Sancta simplicitas!** No need for that!
Swear, without knowing more than you do.

FAUST

Unless you devise a better plan, I'm through!

MEPHISTOPHELES

Saintly fellow! There you go!
Is this the first time that your task
Has been to bear false witness, may I ask?
With brazen brow and dauntless breast,   20
Did you not once expound with power and zest
Meanings of God and of the world, as well
As of all creatures that within it dwell—
Of man, of all that stirs his heart and head?
While if you probe the matter to the core,
You must admit you knew but little more
Than of this Schwerdtlein's death, when all's been said!

FAUST

You were and are a liar, a sophist too.

MEPHISTOPHELES

Yes, did one not take a deeper view.
Tomorrow, in all honor, will not you   30
Delude poor Gretchen and declare
You love her with a love which is divine?

FAUST

With all my heart!

———————

* "Holy simplicity"—here used ironically of Faust's regard for the
truth, which seems naive to Mephisto.

MEPHISTOPHELES

Very good and fine!
Then, eternal faith and love which surge
Like a single overpowering urge—
Will all that flow from your heart still?

FAUST

Enough! When I am stirred, it will, it will!
When into this tumult I am whirled
And for this feeling, this feeling seek a name,   40
Roaming with heightened senses through the world,
Striving for inspiring words, calling this flame
This ecstasy consuming me
Eternal! Unending eternally!
Is that too a devilish lying game?

MEPHISTOPHELES

Yes, I am right!

FAUST

Listen! Take heed,
I beg of you, and let me save my breath!
He who wants to prove he's right, and can talk you to
    death,
Is bound to succeed.   50
But come, this chatter fills me with disgust:
You are right—I admit it since I must.

XII

A GARDEN

MARGARETE *on* FAUST's *arm.* MARTHE *and* MEPHISTOPHELES
walk up and down.

MARGARETE

I'm well aware, sir, that you're sparing me,
Making me feel ashamed by doing so.
Often a traveler good-naturedly
Puts up with what he finds; indeed I know
My simple conversation never can
Appeal to an experienced man.

FAUST

One glance, one word from you appeals far more
Than wisdom and all worldly lore.

(*He kisses her hand.*)

MARGARETE

Don't! How can you kiss my hand? Oh, dear,
It is so rough, so ugly, too!   10
Oh, what work I've had to do!
My mother is really too severe.

(*They pass out of sight.*)

MARTHE

You, sir, are always traveling to and fro?

MEPHISTOPHELES

Business and duty keep us on the go.
We tear ourselves so painfully away
From certain places, yet we dare not stay!

MARTHE

It's all very well when one is young and gay
To knock about the world year after year;
But when, as evil days draw near,
An old bachelor creeps to the grave alone—   20
No one fancies *that*, you'll **own**.

MEPHISTOPHELES

I shudder at the approach of such a fate.

MARTHE

Then, sir, think it over, ere it is too late!

(They pass out of sight.)

MARGARETE

Yes, out of sight is out of mind!
Courtesy comes to you quite naturally;
But surely many friends you find
Cleverer than I could ever be.

FAUST

What passes for cleverness, oh, believe me, sweet,
Is often only narrowness and conceit.

MARGARETE

I don't quite see . . .   30

FAUST

Oh, why are innocence and simplicity
Unknowing of their sacred worth?
Oh, could modesty and humility,
The highest gifts a loving Nature knew—

MARGARETE

Think of me sometimes, just a little while,
I shall have so much time to think of you!

FAUST

Are you then so much alone?

MARGARETE

Yes, although our household's small,
Still, it must be attended to.
We keep no maid; I cook and sweep, and I do all   40
The sewing and knitting that there is to do.
Early and late I hurry so,
For in details my mother is, oh,
So exacting, you know!
Not that she really needs to scrimp this way;
We could afford to spend, better than others may.
My father left us quite a nice estate,
A house and garden near the city gate.
My life goes evenly on day after day;
My brother is a soldier of the King,   50
My baby sister, dead.
I had my troubles with that little thing,
Yet all again I'd gladly do,
She was so dear to me!

FAUST

An angel, if like you!

MARGARETE

I raised her and, oh, she loved me so!
My father died before she came. You know
We thought my mother lost; she lay
So weak and miserable, day by day
Seeming to get her strength back, oh, so slow!   60
Really she could not even try
To nurse the mite, and it was I
Who reared her all alone
On milk and water—thus she was my own.
In my arms or on my lap, the whole day long
She cooed and wriggled, growing strong.

FAUST

You must have felt a deep and pure delight.

MARGARETE

Yet many weary hours as well.
The little cradle stood at night
Beside my bed and I could tell   70
If she but stirred, for I would wake;
Then I'd have to rise, to take
And lay her near me to be fed;
Then, if she'd not be still, get out of bed,
And pace the floor to quiet the little thing.
Early to the wash tubs hurry away,
Then tend the fire, do the marketing,
And ever on, tomorrow like today.
That's why, sir, one's not always at one's best:
But food tastes better for it, so does rest.   80

(They pass out of sight.)

MARTHE

Yes, women get the worst of it! They say
It's hard to make a bachelor change his mind.

MEPHISTOPHELES

It's really up to women of your kind
To train us in a better way.

MARTHE

Speak frankly, sir, are you still fancy-free?
Has your heart not somewhere taken hold?

MEPHISTOPHELES

The proverb says: One's hearth and wife
Are of greater worth than pearls and gold.

MARTHE

Did you never feel desire for anyone, I mean?

MEPHISTOPHELES

I've been politely received, wherever I've been.   90

MARTHE

Were you never really in love, I'm trying to say!

MEPHISTOPHELES

Women should not be trifled with in any way.

MARTHE

Oh, you don't understand!

MEPHISTOPHELES

        I am so blind!
Yet this I understand—you're very kind.

      (They pass out of sight.)

FAUST

Dear child, and so you recognized me
When I came into the garden?

MARGARETE

        Did you not see,
I lowered my eyes.

FAUST

        And you forgive the liberty   100
I took, and my impertinence—
For you had barely left the cathedral door!

MARGARETE

I was so upset! This never happened before;
No one ever spoke of me in an evil sense.
Oh, could he have seen—to myself I said—
Something improper, something bold in you?
For right away he takes it into his head
He can handle this wench the way he wishes to!
I must own up, something—I don't know why—
Was stirring in your favor from the start.   110
I felt so angry with myself that I
Could not be angrier with you in my heart!

FAUST

Dear love!

MARGARETE

Wait!

(*She picks a daisy and plucks off the petals one by one.*)

FAUST

What's that for? A bouquet?

MARGARETE

No, it's a game.

FAUST

How?

MARGARETE

You'll laugh at me! Go away!

(*She pulls off the petals, murmuring to herself.*)

FAUST

What are you murmuring?

MARGARETE (*half aloud*)

He loves me—loves me not. 120

FAUST

Blessèd angel!

MARGARETE (*continuing aloud*)

Loves me—not—loves me—not—

(*Pulling off the last petal with pure delight*)

He loves me!

FAUST

Yes, child! Oh, let this flower's words
Be God's affirmation! He loves you!
Ah, do you know what that means? He loves you!

(*He grasps both her hands.*)

MARGARETE

I'm trembling through and through!

FAUST

Oh, do not shudder! Let my eyes,
The touch of my hands reveal to you this,
This—that cannot be expressed: 130
To yield oneself completely, to feel
A joy which must be endless!
Endless! The end would mean despair!
No, no end!—no end!

(MARGARETE *presses his hands, frees herself, and runs off.*
FAUST *stands for a moment in thought, then follows her.*)

MARTHE (*coming forward*)

The night draws on.

MEPHISTOPHELES

We must be on our way.

MARTHE

I'd ask you gentlemen to stay,
But this is much too mean a place for you.
People here have nothing else to do
Or think of, day in, day out,   140
Than tag their neighbor's steps and stare.
No matter how one acts, one gets so talked about.
And our young pair?

MEPHISTOPHELES

        Flew up the path just there.
Playful birds!

MARTHE

He seems to take to her.

MEPHISTOPHELES

And she to him. That's the way of the world.

XIII

A SUMMER HOUSE

MARGARETE *runs in, hides behind the door, puts her finger-tips to her lips, and peeps through the crack.*

MARGARETE

He's coming!

        (FAUST *enters.*)

FAUST

You rogue! So you are teasing me!
If I catch you!

(*He kisses her.*)

MARGARETE (*embracing him and returning his kiss*)

I love you, dearest one, with all my heart!

(MEPHISTOPHELES *begins to knock.*)

FAUST (*stamping his foot*)

Who's there?

MEPHISTOPHELES

A friend!

FAUST

A beast!

MEPHISTOPHELES

It's time to part.

(MARTHE *enters.*)

MARTHE

Yes, sir, it's late.

FAUST

May I take you across the way?   10

MARGARETE

Oh, what would my mother say!
Good-bye!

FAUST

Must I really go?
Then good-bye, my sweet.

MARTHE

Good-bye, sir.

MARGARETE

Till next we meet.

(*Exeunt* FAUST *and* MEPHISTOPHELES.)

Heavens! To think a man could so
Know everything there is to know!
I stand before him blushing red,
And just say "Yes" to all he's said.   20
What a child I am! I cannot see
What he ever finds in me!

(*Exit.*)

XIV

FOREST AND CAVERN

FAUST (*alone*)

Sublime Spirit, thou hast given me all,
All for which I besought thee. Not in vain
Didst thou reveal thy countenance in the fire.
Thou hast given me Nature for a kingdom,
With strength to enjoy and feel. Thou didst
Not only permit me a visit of cold amazement,
Thou didst allow me to peer into her deep breast
As into the heart of a friend. Before my eyes

Thou didst lead the ranks of living creatures,
Teaching me to know my brothers in the air,   10
In the deep waters and in the silent coverts.
When through the forest the storm rattles and rages,
Uprooting the giant pines which in their fall,
Crashing, drag down neighboring boughs and trunks
Whose ruin makes hollow thunder shake the hills;
Then thou dost lead me into a sheltering cave,
And revealest me to myself and layest bare
The deep mysterious miracle of my nature.
And when the pure moon rises into sight
Soothingly above me, then about me hover,   20
Creeping from rocky walls and dewy thickets,
Silver shadows, phantoms of a bygone world,
Which allay the austere joy of meditation.
Now fully do I realize man can never
Possess perfection! With this rapture
Which brings me near and nearer to the gods,
Thou gavest me this comrade whom I now
Cannot dispense with, though cold and insolent;
He lowers me in my own regard and can transform
Thy gifts to nothingness by one faint word.   30
Within my breast assiduously he fans
The flame of longing for that lovely image.
Thus from desire I stagger to enjoyment,
And in enjoyment languish for desire.

(MEPHISTOPHELES *enters.*)

MEPHISTOPHELES

Come, come, have you not had your fill
Of this life yet? Can you enjoy it still?
It's all very well if you have tried
It once. But then go on to something new!

FAUST

I wish that you had something else to do
Than pester me when I am satisfied.   40

MEPHISTOPHELES

There, there, I'll gladly let you be!
But you don't dare to say it seriously.
A comrade so unstable, rude, and cross
Is really very little loss.
One has one's hands full all day long,
Yet, from the looks of him, one cannot tell
What to say or what to leave alone.

FAUST

What an extraordinary tone!
He bores me, yet he asks for thanks as well.

MEPHISTOPHELES

Poor earthly creature! How, I'd like to know,   50
Could you have lived your life without my aid?
At least I cured you long ago
From the flimflam your phantasy had made;
And, if I had not been here,
You would have rambled off this sphere.
What are you doing in these cliffs and caves,
Like a moping owl, perched here alone?
What are you sucking, like a toad which craves
Nourishment from soggy moss and dripping stone?
A lovely pastime to dabble in!   60
Still the same Professor beneath the skin!

FAUST

Can you not grasp what fresh vitality
This living in the wilderness has wrought in me?

I do believe, if you could guess,
You'd be Devil enough to grudge this happiness.

MEPHISTOPHELES

What a supernatural delight!
To lie in the night dew on the mountain height,
Clasping earth and heaven in rapture! To inflate
Your being to a godlike state,
Burrowing through the earth with yearning urge,   70
Feeling in your heart the six-day creative surge,
Enjoying I know not what with power and pride,
The earthly self completely cast aside,
And flooding all with love's deep ecstasy,
Then the lofty intuition—

(*With a gesture*)

                              Hm—well, you see
I dare not mention what the end should be!

FAUST

For shame!

MEPHISTOPHELES

            You don't like it, eh? So you claim
The moral right to cry out, "Shame!"   80
Before chaste ears one cannot talk about
Some things which chaste hearts cannot do without.
Well, I do not begrudge your pleasure when
You lie to yourself a little now and then.
You cannot keep this up for long; indeed,
You are again distracted, and it's plain
If this continues it will lead
To horror, anxiety, or drive you insane.
Enough of this! Your sweetheart sits at home,
And life to her has a drab and dreary hue.   90

You never leave her thoughts at all,
She's overpoweringly in love with you.
First your passion rose to overflow,
As when a brook is swelled by melting snow;
You poured it all into her heart, and sigh
Because your little stream is running dry.
It seems to me, instead of playing king
In these woods, your lordship could afford
To give the poor young silly thing,
For all her love and longing, some reward.   100
Time hangs so heavily upon her hands;
At her window, watching the clouds drifting o'er
The ancient city walls, idly she stands.
"Oh, were I a bird!" So runs her song,
Half through the night and all day long.
Sometimes she's cheerful, often she sighs,
Sometimes she cries and cries,
Then is calm again, or seems to be;
For always utterly in love is she!

FAUST

Serpent! Serpent!   110

MEPHISTOPHELES (*aside*)

Ha! There I have you!

FAUST

Infamous wretch! Away! Away!
Do not mention that belovèd girl!
Do not prick my tortured senses into pain
With craving for her lovely body again.

MEPHISTOPHELES

What then? She thinks you've flown. Come, confess,
This is what you have done, more or less!

FAUST

Though I were far, I'm near to her somehow,
I'll never forget her, never lose her now!
Yes, I even envy the Host   120
When her lips touch it!

MEPHISTOPHELES

                    Very, very fine indeed!
My friend, I've often envied you
Those twins which 'midst the roses feed.

FAUST

Begone, pander!

MEPHISTOPHELES

                    You rail, but I laugh! In truth,
The God who fashioned maid and youth
Realized the noblest calling to be
The power of creating opportunity.
It really is a pity— Let's be off!   130
You should be going to your sweetheart's room,
Not to your doom.

FAUST

What though the joy of Heaven lies in her arms? What
      though
I warm myself against her breast?
Do I not always feel her woe?
Am I not an outcast? a fugitive?
A monster without purpose, without rest,
That, like a cataract from rock to rock leaping,
Plunges into the abyss, in greedy anger sweeping?
Whilst she, with childlike feeling, lived   140

In a cottage near an Alpine field;
There the modest home life was begun,
Within her little world concealed.
And I, whom God abhors,
Oh, was it not enough, enough,
When I embraced the rocks to blast
Them into fragments at the last?
Her peace I had to undermine as well!
You claimed this victim, merciless Hell!
Help, Fiend, curtail this time of misery!   150
Let what must happen, happen without delay!
Let her fate come crashing down on me,
Let us sink together to our doom!

MEPHISTOPHELES

Again he seethes, again he glows!
Go in, you fool, and comfort her!
When a pinhead such as you no exit knows,
He thinks the end must speedily occur.
Long life to the valiant everywhere!
You're fairly well bedeviled otherwise.
There's nothing in the world I so despise   160
As a devil in despair.

XV

GRETCHEN'S ROOM

GRETCHEN (*alone, at the spinning-wheel*)

My peace has fled,
    My heart is sore,
I never shall find it,
    Ah, nevermore!

My life is a grave
    When he is not near,
And all the world
    Is bitter and drear.

Oh, my poor head
    Is so puzzled, so crazed,   10
My reason and senses
    Are utterly dazed!

My peace has fled,
    My heart is sore,
I never shall find it,
    Ah, nevermore!

Just to see him I stay
    At the window late;
Just to see him I hurry
    Forth to the gate.   20

His bearing, his manner,
    Distinguished and wise,
The smile on his lips,
    The fire in his eyes,

His words, like the flow
    Of magical bliss,
His hand meeting mine,
    Then . . . his kiss!

My peace has fled,
    My heart is sore,   30
I never shall find it,
    Ah, nevermore!

My being, in longing,
>Follows him ever,
Ah, could I clasp him,
>Mine only, forever!

Ah, could I then—
>As my heart urges, be
Lost in kisses
>Of ecstasy!   40

XVI

MARTHE'S GARDEN

MARGARETE   FAUST

MARGARETE

Answer me truly, dear love!

FAUST

If I can.

MARGARETE

Tell me, dear, in what you do believe! Although
You are a good and loveworthy man,
Religion means little to you, that I know.

FAUST

Let that be, my child! You feel my love, is it not true?
For those I love, I'd lay my life down too;
I would rob no one of his faith and trust.

MARGARETE

That's not enough! One must believe, one must!

FAUST

Must one?   10

MARGARETE

Ah, had I some influence over you!
Neither do you revere the Sacrament.

FAUST

I revere it.

MARGARETE

Without desiring it, I meant.
Nor were you at Mass or confession for an age.
Do you believe in God?

FAUST

Who'd dare to say,
"I believe in God"? Sweetheart, you may
Ask priest or sage,
The answer which you would receive   20
Would seem to mock the seeker.

MARGARETE

Then you do not believe?

FAUST

Do not misunderstand me, blessèd one!
Who dares to name Him?
Who can acclaim Him,
Saying, "Yes, I believe in Him"?
Experiencing Him everywhere,
Who would dare
To say, "I do not believe in Him"?
The All-enfolding,   30

The All-sustaining,
Does He not enfold and uphold
You—me—Himself?
Does not the earth lie firm beneath?
Do not the heavens arch above?
Do not eternal stars ascend,
Nodding with friendly light and love?
Do we not look deeply into each other's eyes,
Does not a flow of feeling start
Sweeping through you from head to heart,   40
Weaving its eternal mystery
Round you visibly, invisibly?
Let its vastness suffuse and fill
Your heart! When in this feeling wholly blessed,
Then call it what you will!
Call it Happiness! Heart! Love! God!
I have no name for it!
Feeling is all!
The name is only sound and smoke
Which fogs the glow of Heaven.   50

MARGARETE

Yes, that's all very well and good;
The priest says pretty much the same,
In different words, or so I've understood.

FAUST

All hearts in all places say
The same, beneath the blessèd light of day,
Each in his own words and way;
So why not I in mine?

MARGARETE

It sounds plausible when you put it so;
There's something not quite straight about it, though!
You've no sound Christianity.   60

FAUST

Dear child!

MARGARETE

I have been sick at heart to see
You keeping such company.

FAUST

How so?

MARGARETE

That man you take about with you
Is hateful to my very soul.
In all my life I never knew
Aught could stab me so deeply as a glance
From his repulsive countenance.

FAUST

Darling, do not fear him—you must not mind.   70

MARGARETE

My blood runs cold when he draws near.
Otherwise, to everyone I'm kind.
But, much as I long to see you, dear,
At sight of him I'm filled with secret fear!
That he's a scoundrel is plain as plain can be!
If I do him injustice—God pardon me!

FAUST

Such queer fish must also be.

MARGARETE

I would not want to live with such as he!
When, as it's happened, he steps inside our door,
He always peers about so sneeringly,   80

Half-infuriated! One can see
He has no interest, no, not in anything! What's more,
Upon his brow it's stamped quite clear
He is incapable of love.
Ah, in your arms enfolded—happy here—
I am so wholly yours, so warm, so free!
But his mere presence stifles me.

FAUST

Intuitive child!

MARGARETE

        This overpowers me so, that when
He meets us casually any day,   90
I feel I do not love you! . . . Then,
When he is near I cannot pray,
And this eats out my heart with pain;
Surely, dearest, surely you feel the same!

FAUST

There, there, it's just an antipathy!

MARGARETE

Now I must go.

FAUST

        Ah, shall I never rest
An hour quietly upon your breast,
Heart to heart and soul to soul, my own?

MARGARETE

Oh, if only I slept alone!   100
Gladly I'd leave the door unlatched tonight,
But mother sleeps so very light;

And, were she to find us, like as not
I should be dead upon the spot!

FAUST

My darling, do not be afraid.
Take this little phial! Pour
Three drops only in her glass, no more,
Then nature with deepest slumber us will aid.

MARGARETE

For your sake, what do I not do!
It will not harm her if I should?   110

FAUST

Would I suggest it, sweetheart, if it could?

MARGARETE

When I but see you, love, ah, then I do
Not know what power drives me to your will;
Already I have done so much for you,
Little is left me to fulfill!

(Exit.)

(MEPHISTOPHELES *enters.*)

MEPHISTOPHELES

The pert young thing! Has she gone?

FAUST

Were you spying again?

MEPHISTOPHELES

I took it all in, and was most surprised
To hear the Professor roundly catechized;
Let's hope it agrees! All girls appear   120

Very interested to find out
Whether a man is orthodox and devout.
They think: he knuckled there, he'll truckle here.

FAUST

You, monster, fail to see
How this young girl, so pure and true
(Imbued with a deeply earnest faith
Which to her means her soul's salvation),
Torments herself with doubts lest she
Admit her dear love destined for damnation!

MEPHISTOPHELES

You supersensual, sensual lover,   130
A girl is making a fool of you!

FAUST

Misbegotten creature of filth and flame!

MEPHISTOPHELES

We've here an expert in physiognomy.
She feels she scarce knows what—close to me!
My outer mask augurs some secret thought,
She's convinced I am a Genius of a sort,
Perhaps the Devil himself!
As for tonight—

FAUST

What's that to do with you?

MEPHISTOPHELES

Hm, I have my pleasure in it too!   140

XVII

AT THE WELL

GRETCHEN *and* LIESCHEN *with jugs*

LIESCHEN

Have you heard about Barbara, by the way?

GRETCHEN

No, I see few people.

LIESCHEN

            It's true, though, what they say,
Sibylle told me so today!
At last she has been duped for fair;
That's what comes of her grand air!

GRETCHEN

What do you mean?

LIESCHEN

            I'll tell it straight to you:
Whenever she eats and drinks, she's feeding two!

GRETCHEN

Oh!   10

LIESCHEN

    It serves her right!
How long she hung around that fellow! 'Twas a sight
To see them promenading up and down,
Now to the dance place, now through the town,
And she the first one everywhere,

And he, treating to cakes and wine, until I swear
She grew so vain about her pretty face,
She lowered herself and thought it no disgrace
To take his gifts. Well, such a to-do!
Such billing and cooing!   20
Then the flower was plucked before one knew!

                    GRETCHEN

Oh, the poor thing!

                    LIESCHEN

                You need not pity *her!*
Whilst we girls from our spinning could not stir,
And nights our mothers kept us home,
She went gadding with her beau alone;
On the door bench, in the dark passageway,
For them no hour was too late to stay.
Now, however, she'll have to hang her head,
And do penance in a sinner's shirt, instead!   30

                    GRETCHEN

Surely he'll marry her!

                    LIESCHEN

                He'd be a fool! What for?
So clever a chap has chances everywhere.
Besides, he's gone.

                    GRETCHEN

                But that's not fair!

                    LIESCHEN

If she gets him she had best look out.
The boys will snatch her wreath, and at the door
We will scatter chaff about.   *(Exit.)*

GRETCHEN (*going home*)

How I once railed, in what a cruel way,
When some poor girl had gone astray!   40
I scarce found words enough to blame
And talk of someone else's sin and shame!
Black though it was, blacker it had to be,
Yet it was never black enough for me.
I blessed my stars, held my head high,
And now—now the living sin am I!
Yet all that drove me on to this, I knew
Only as sweet, only as true!

XVIII

CITADEL

*In a niche of the wall is a shrine with a devotional picture
of the Mater Dolorosa. Vases for flowers are placed before it.*

GRETCHEN (*putting fresh flowers in the vases*)

Mother of Sorrows,
Bend down to me,
And look with pity and mercy on my distress!

A sword is piercing Thy heart,
And, racked by agony,
Thou art looking up to where Thy Son lies dead.

Thou art looking up to the Father, and Thy sigh
Ascends on high,
Because of His grief and Thy despair and dread.

But who can feel   10
The pain now torturing me
Unceasingly?
Why my heart's in anguish here,
All its longing, all its fear,
Thou and Thou alone canst know.

Whate'er I do, where'er I go,
How bitter the woe
Harrowing my breast!
And when I am alone again
I weep and weep and weep,   20
Breaking my heart in pain.

With tears the flowers 'neath my window
Are watered bitterly,
As at dawn I gather them
To bring to Thee.

For when the sun with early light
Creeps into my little room,
It finds me up and seated on my bed,
Lost in misery and dread.

Help me! Save me from shame and death!   30
Mother of Sorrows,
Bend down to me,
And look with pity and mercy on my distress!

XIX

NIGHT

Street before GRETCHEN'S *door*

VALENTIN, *a soldier and* GRETCHEN'S *brother*

VALENTIN

When I'd sit drinking with the men,
Where certain fellows like to boast
About their pick of girls and then
With brimming glasses drain a toast—
On elbows leaning, I'd attend
To all their bunkum to the end;
Sitting in quiet unconcern,
I'd stroke my beard and smiling turn
And seize the full glass, close at hand,
And say: "Each to his taste! But where,   10
Can one be found in all the land
Who can in any way compare
With my own Gretchen? Come now—say!
Who matches my sister in any way?"
Clink! Clink! "To her!" the round would fly,
And some "The fellow's right!" would cry,
"She's the flower of her sex, I swear!"
Dumb sat the braggarts one and all.
But now—oh, I could tear my hair,
And dash my head against the wall!   20
With a taunting sneer, nose in the air,
Each scamp has the laugh on me! Whilst I
Like a sorry debtor sit and sweat,
Flinching as chance remarks fly by.
I could bang their heads together, and yet
I cannot tell them that they lie.

What's coming here? Who's sneaking up?
Unless I am mistaken, two appear.
If he's the one, I'll seize him by the throat!
He'll never get away alive from here! 30

FAUST   MEPHISTOPHELES

FAUST

As from the window of the sacristy, the light
Of the ever-living lamp is found
To flicker, then grow less and still less bright,
While darkness slowly closes in around—
So in my breast the dismal shadows close.

MEPHISTOPHELES

Whilst I feel like a yearning cat which goes
Down the fire ladders, slinking by,
Meandering along the walls, stealthily sly.
I feel quite virtuous, I do,
A bit thievish, a bit lustful too, 40
As down my limbs run thrills of pure delight,
Precursors of Walpurgis Night.
Two days hence, the hour's at hand; then no mistake,
You'll know the reason why one stays awake.

FAUST

Will not that treasure soon rise plain to sight
Which I see yonder, as a flickering light?

MEPHISTOPHELES

Very shortly you will know the fun
Of lifting up a pot of gold;
I peeped a while ago in one;
Some splendid coins it seemed to hold. 50

FAUST

But was there not an ornament, a ring?
Some trifle to adorn my girl?

MEPHISTOPHELES

Indeed, 'twixt other stuff I saw something
Which might have been a string of pearls.

FAUST

Good! It really hurts me if I go
Tonight without a present to display.

MEPHISTOPHELES

Pleasure for which you do not pay
Ought really not to vex you so.
Now that with stars the sky is brightly lit,
You'll hear a very masterpiece of song:
I'll sing her first a moral bit,
The better to jolly her along.

(*He sings, accompanying himself on the zither.*)

   Katrinka dear!
   What dost thou here,
   As dawn grows near,
   Outside thy lover's door?
   I'd be afraid!
   He'll let thee in a maid,
   But out a maid
   Thou'lt not come any more. 70

   Beware! Beware!
   Once his, my fair,
   For adieux prepare,
   Poor silly thing!

Though ye love each other, be
Not, for love's sake, too free
With a heartbreaker—save he
Brings first the wedding ring.

VALENTIN (*coming forward*)

Whom are you decoying? God's Element!
You damnable, piping ratcatcher!   80
First to the Devil, the instrument!
Then to the Devil, the singer!

MEPHISTOPHELES

You've smashed the zither! Now it's fit
For naught!

VALENTIN

Next there is a skull to split!

MEPHISTOPHELES (*to* FAUST)

Don't flinch, Professor! Just keep cool, stand pat!
Follow as I lead. . . . Stick close to me.
Out with your skewer! See—
You lunge, I parry!

VALENTIN

Parry *that!*   90

MEPHISTOPHELES

Why not? I'm only just commencing!

VALENTIN

And that!

MEPHISTOPHELES

Of course!

VALENTIN

>   The Devil must be fencing!
> What's this? My hand's already lamed!

MEPHISTOPHELES (*to* FAUST)

> Thrust home!

VALENTIN (*falls*)

>   O God!

MEPHISTOPHELES

>   There—the lout is tamed!
> Quick, let's be off! It's time to disappear;
> Already they are shouting murder here.   100
> With the police I get on without fail,
> But penal law is quite another tale!

(*Exit with* FAUST.)

MARTHE (*at the window*)

> Come out! Come out!

GRETCHEN (*at the window*)

>   A light! A light!

MARTHE (*as above*)

> They're shrieking, scuffling, swearing—it's a fight.

THE CROWD

> One is lying there already dead!

MARTHE (*coming out*)

> Where have the murderers fled?

GRETCHEN (*coming out*)

Who's lying here?

THE CROWD

Your mother's son.

GRETCHEN

Almighty God! What have they done?   110

VALENTIN

I'm dying! That is quickly said,
More quickly done. Look here,
Why do you women weep and wail? Instead,
Listen to what I have to say—draw near!

(*All crowd around him.*)

My Gretchen! Although still young, my dear,
You are not worldly-wise enough, I fear;
You manage all your business wrong.
I'll tell you this in confidence: so long
As you're a whore, since you've begun,
Become one outright and be done!   120

GRETCHEN

My brother! God! What do you mean?

VALENTIN

Leave God out of this scene!
I tell you what is past is past,
What follows now will follow fast.
You started secretly with one,
Others will come, now you've begun,
And when you've had a dozen men,
All the town can have you then.

When shame into the world is born,
She comes clandestinely 'midst tears,   130
Softly the veil of night is drawn
Around her head and ears;
One longs to kill her! But when she grows,
And power arrogantly shows,
Brazenly she struts by day,
Yet is no handsomer in any way.
The uglier she is to sight,
The more she seeks the broad daylight.

I see the hour drawing near
When every honest person here,   140
From you, harlot! will turn away
As from a body in decay.
Your guilty heart will burn you through
When people merely look at you!
Never will you wear a fine gold chain,
Nor at the altar take your place;
Wearing a collar of the finest lace,
Never will you enjoy a dance again!
But in some corner, cast aside
Among cripples and beggars, you will hide;   150
Even though God Himself forgive,
May you be damned on earth!

MARTHE

Commend your soul to God's good will!
Must you to your sins add blasphemy?

VALENTIN

If only I could reach your withered frame,
Vile procuress, you base thing of shame!
Ah, then I could have hope to win
Pardon in full for every sin!

GRETCHEN

My brother! This is the agony of Hell!

VALENTIN

Dry those useless tears, I say!   160
When you flung your honor away,
You dealt my heart its fatal blow.
Now through the sleep of death I go
To God, a soldier to the end!

(*He dies.*)

XX

IN THE CATHEDRAL

Mass with choir and organ.

GRETCHEN *amongst a crowd of people. The* EVIL SPIRIT *behind* GRETCHEN.

THE EVIL SPIRIT

How different, Gretchen,
How different you were
When here to the altar you came,
So innocent, so chaste,
Murmuring your prayers
From the worn, befingered little book,
Half like a child,
Half stirred by God!
Gretchen!
Where are your thoughts?   10
And in your heart

What terrible crime?
Are you praying for the soul of your mother,
Which through your doing
Passed in sleep down, down into unending torment?
Whose blood is staining your doorstep?
And beneath your heart,
Is not something stirring into life
Whose ill-boding presence tortures itself and you?

GRETCHEN

O God! O God!   20
Were I but free from thoughts
Which float above and about me
Despite my will!

CHOIR

Dies irae, dies illa
*Solvet saeclum in favilla.**

(Organ music)

THE EVIL SPIRIT

The wrath of doom seizes you!
The last trumpet sounds!
The graves quiver and quake!
Out of the quiet ashes of death
Your heart is requickened,   30
Only to be plunged once more
Into flames of torment!

---

*"Day of wrath, when the world shall crumble in ashes." The text
goes on (see next page): "When the Judge shall sit in judgment and
all that is hidden shall appear and no crime shall go unpunished.
What then shall I, poor sinner, say in my defense; whom shall I call
on for help, when even the righteous shall tremble?" (Parts of the
famous sequence attributed to Thomas of Celano, thirteenth century,
and used in the Mass for the Dead.)

GRETCHEN

Oh, were I away from here!
I feel the organ
Is robbing me of breath,
The chant dissolving
My inmost heart.

CHOIR

Judex ergo cum sedebit,
Quidquid latet, adparebit,
Nil inultum remanebit. 40

GRETCHEN

I cannot breathe!
The pillars imprison me!
The vaulted arch
Presses down upon me!
Air! . . . Air!

THE EVIL SPIRIT

Hide yourself, Gretchen!
Sin and shame
Never remain concealed.
Light? Air?
Woe upon you! 50

CHOIR

Quid sum miser tunc dicturus,
Quem patronum rogaturus,
Cum vix justus sit securus?

THE EVIL SPIRIT

The Glorified turn
Their faces away.

The Pure shudder
At offering you their hands.
Woe! Woe!

CHOIR

Quid sum miser tunc dicturus?

GRETCHEN

Neighbor! Help me . . . I'm fainting!   60

(*She falls to the floor in a faint.*)

XXI

WALPURGIS NIGHT

The Harz Mountains
Vicinity of Schierke and Elend

FAUST   MEPHISTOPHELES

MEPHISTOPHELES

Would you not like a broomstick? I would say
Give me a he-goat, rough and strong!
Our goal by this road still is far away.

FAUST

This knotted stick suffices me so long
As I feel fresh upon my legs.
Why take the shorter cut? To me it seems
That creeping through this labyrinthine vale,
Next these rocky cliffs to scale,
Whence from its source trickling water streams.

Is the pleasure which to such a walk lends zest! 10
Spring quickens the birches; one can tell
The fir trees feel its power as do the rest.
Why should it not affect our limbs as well?

MEPHISTOPHELES

It does not touch me in the least!
My body feels wintry yet, and chill;
I long for frost and snow upon our path.
How sadly the imperfect disc of the red moon still
Is rising with belated glow;
So faint a light it seems to throw
That at each step one strikes a rock or tree. 20
Let me summon a will-o'-the-wisp; I see
One burning brightly over there;
Ho, friend! Will you not aid us with your light?
Why keep on flickering this useless flare?
Be good enough to guide us up the height!

THE WILL-O'-THE-WISP

Out of respect I hope I can subdue
My fickle nature, and submit to you;
Usually our pace is a zigzag gait.

MEPHISTOPHELES

Ho! Ho! Is't man he would imitate?
Go straight, in the Devil's name! 30
Else I will blow out your flickering flame.

THE WILL-O'-THE-WISP

I will adapt myself to you as best I can,
Since you are master here. Bear in mind this fact:
The mountain is bewitched today,
And if a will-o'-the-wisp must light your way,
You must not ask it to be too exact.

FAUST, MEPHISTOPHELES, WILL-O'-THE-WISP

(*In alternating song*)

Since it seems we've been admitted
To these dreamlike magic spaces,
Guide us nicely through these places,
So that soon we be permitted   40
In the vast and desolate regions.

Watch the trees like forest legions,
Passing by and swift descending,
While the cliffs keep bowing, bending,
And the rocks, long-snouted fellows—
How each snorts, and how each bellows!

Over stones, through meadows growing,
Down rush brook and brooklet flowing.
Do I hear rustling? Do I hear singing?
Songs in which the heart rejoices,   50
Like those tender heavenly voices
Which we love and, loving, hail,
While faint Echo, like a tale
Of olden, golden days, is ringing?

Tu-whit! Tu-whoo! Not far away
Cry plover, screech owl, and the jay
Did they remain awake today?
Does the lanky, paunchy salamander,
Through the tangled bush meander?
How the roots, like serpents winding   60
Out of rocks and sand dunes, linger,
Stretching tendrils like a finger,
Us to frighten—coiling, binding!
From the living, knotted gnarls,
Polypus feelers stretch their snarls

Toward the wanderer. Mice are scurrying,
Mice of thousand colors, hurrying,
Scuffling through the moss and heather!
And the fireflies are gleaming,
Flying, crowding, pushing, streaming—   70
Bewild'ring escorts, flocked together!

Tell me, then, if we are waiting,
Or if onward we are going?
All is whirling, rushing, blowing,
Trees and rocks are making faces,
Will-o'-the-wisps with arts and graces
Are augmenting and dilating.

MEPHISTOPHELES

Come now, clutch my mantle tightly!
Here a middle peak is showing,
Whence, astonished, one sees brightly   80
Mammon in the mountains glowing.

FAUST

Mysteriously through yawning chasms gleams
A murky reddish tinge like break of day!
Into the deepest crevices it seems
To scent and pick its way!
There rises steam, there vapor drifts from sight,
From mist and film flickers a glowing light;
Yonder like a slender thread it creeps,
Then like a rustling spring which sweeps
On its course with foaming zest   90
Into the valley, in hundred veins, to left and right,
While here, into a corner pressed,
Suddenly the streams unite.
Near by flashing sparks of light
Are scattering like golden sands.

But look—in all its splendid height,
Ablaze the rocky precipice stands!

MEPHISTOPHELES

Does not Sir Mammon illuminate
His halls in splendor for this fete?
What luck you've seen it! Hush! I hear   100
The boisterous guests, drawing near.

FAUST

How the wind storm races through the air!
It beats upon my neck with blow on blow!

MEPHISTOPHELES

Cling to the old ribs of the rock—take care,
Else you'll be hurled into the abyss below!
A heavy mist darkens the night.
Hear the crashing of trees! In fright,
Away the terrified owls flit.
Listen! The columns splinter and split
In the evergreen hall!   110
Branches crack and fall!
The tree trunks moan!
The roots creak and groan!
Snarled and tangled hideously,
Tree crashes heavily into tree,
While o'er the stormy wreck-strewn cliffs
Hiss and howl the violent winds!
D'you hear voices on the height?
Far away? nearer me?
A frenzied song of sorcery   120
Is sweeping the mountain crest tonight!

WITCHES (*in chorus*)

The witches ride to the Brocken Horn,
The stubble is yellow, green the corn!

The rabble is gathered, awaiting the call,
Aloft sits Sir Urian* ruling them all.
On they go, over stick, over stone;
The he-goat stinks and also the crone.

A VOICE

Alone Old Baubo† is coming now,
Riding astride a farrow-sow.

CHORUS

Honor to whom all honors belong!   130
Dame Baubo, forward! Lead the throng!
A good old sow, the mother atop!
Witches following, neck and crop!

A VOICE

Which way did you come?

ANOTHER VOICE

O'er Ilsenstein crest!
I peeked into an owlet's nest,
She lowered and glowered!

ANOTHER VOICE

Oh, go to Hell!
Why d'you gallop like this, pell-mell!

A VOICE

See, she has hurt me as she flew by,   140
Jostled and bruised me, shoulder and thigh!

WITCHES (*in chorus*)

The way is broad, the way is long,
Was there ever such a crazy throng?

---

* Another name for the devil.
† Demeter's nurse, byword for a leader of obscene revels.

The broomstick scratches, the pitchfork pokes,
The mother bursts, the infant chokes!

WIZARDS (*semi-chorus*)

We creep along like a snail in its house,
And by the women we are led;
For when it concerns the Devil's house,
Woman is a thousand steps ahead.

OTHER SEMI-CHORUS

Such fine distinctions we don't make,   150
Woman a thousand steps may take;
But, much as she hurries to cover the ground,
Man arrives with a single bound.

A VOICE (*above*)

Ho there, from the Felsensee! Come up! Oh, do!

A VOICE (*below*)

We'd gladly climb the heights with you.
We've washed until we can't scrub more;
Yet we're as sterile as before.

BOTH CHORUSES

The wind is hushed, the stars now die,
The murky moon hides in the sky,
While crowds of wizards whizzing by   160
Make sparks of sputtering fire fly.

A VOICE (*below*)

Stop! Stop! Oh, don't let me be left!

A VOICE (*above*)

Who's calling out of the rocky cleft?

A VOICE (*below*)

Take me with you! Oh, please stop!
I've struggled up three hundred years,
Yet I can never reach the top.
I'd like to be amongst my peers.

BOTH CHORUSES

A broomstick carries you, so will a stick,
A pitchfork carries you, a goat does the trick;
He who cannot raise himself today,   170
Lost forevermore must stay.

A HALF-WITCH (*below*)

I've stumbled on till I'm half dead;
How did the others get far ahead?
For peace at home there is no chance,
And here I never shall advance.

CHORUS OF WITCHES

This salve gives courage to a hag,
For a sail she takes a bit of rag,
A ship is fashioned from a bough;
He never will fly who can't fly now.

BOTH CHORUSES

When we have circled the summit around,   180
Lightly trail along the ground,
And in bewitching coveys glide
To cover the heath from far and wide.

(*They alight.*)

MEPHISTOPHELES

They crowd and they jostle, they rattle and clatter!
They hiss and they whirl, they bustle and chatter!

They sparkle and spirt, they stink and they burn!
A real witch-element, as you shall learn!
Hold on to me! Else we'll be parted in turn.
Where are you?

FAUST (*in the distance*)

      Here!   190

MEPHISTOPHELES

          What! Thrust out of sight?
I must step in—asserting my right.
Room for Sir Voland!* Sweet rabble, give ground!
Doctor, your hand! Then with a bound
Out of this crowd we'll skip easily;
It's too crazy even for the likes of me!
Close by in those bushes, a curious glow
Draws me thither. Come, let's go!
Behind them we will disappear.

FAUST

Spirit of Contradiction! Lead!   200
Forward! You manage cleverly indeed;
So we walk to the Brocken on Walpurgis Night,
To enjoy our solitude upon its height!

MEPHISTOPHELES

Look, what varicolored flames burn bright!
Here is a club with quite a lively tone;
In little circles one is not alone.

FAUST

Yet higher up I'd like to go—
Already I see a whirling, smoky glow.

---

* Still another name for the devil.

To the Evil One, crowds are streaming from each side;
There many a knotty riddle must be untied.   210

MEPHISTOPHELES

There also many a riddle knottily tied.
Let the vast world rumble on and riot,
Here let us house ourselves in quiet.
Long ago 'twas known and plainly stated
That, in the great world, small worlds are created.
See those young and naked witches there,
And clever old ones who do not go bare.
For my sake do be friendly to them all,
The fun is great, the cost is small.
I hear the fiddles being tuned up now!   220
Damned twanging! One must grow used to such a row.
Come on! Come on! It has to be!
I'll enter first and lead you in with me,
And show you something different in this place.
What say you, friend? This is no tiny space!
You scarcely see the end! Just think,
A hundred fires burning in a row; they drink,
They cook, they chatter, dance and kiss:
Tell me, pray, is anything better than this?

FAUST

To introduce us, will you devise   230
A wizard or a devil's guise?

MEPHISTOPHELES

Though incognito usually I go,
On gala days my insignia must show.
The garter is not one of them; in truth,
Here they revere the cloven hoof.
D'you see that snail which creeps about?
Groping with feelers just like eyes,

It has already sniffed me out.
Try as I would here, they'd see through my disguise.
But come! We'll go from fire to fire,   240
I, the go-between—you, the squire.

(*To a few people who are sitting around some dying
embers*)

Oldsters, why sit upon the periphery
Of pleasure? I'd praise you, did I see you taking
Leading roles in this youthful merrymaking;
One is long enough at home in quiet.

A GENERAL

What faith can man have in his nation!
He spends himself upon his native land,
Yet with the people, just as with a woman,
Youth forever gains the upper hand.

A MINISTER

I sing and roundly praise the good old times,   250
Now they're far from all that's wise and sage,
But the day we were in power,
That was the veritable Golden Age.

A PARVENU

We were not altogether stupid men,
Though, I admit it, we oft did err;
Now topsy-turvy are the times,
Just when we'd like to keep things as they were.

AN AUTHOR

In these days who would ever read
A book of sense and substance anyhow!
As for the younger generation,   260
They never were as impudent as now.

MEPHISTOPHELES (*who suddenly appears very old*)

I feel that men are ripe for judgment day,
The witches' hill a last time I ascend;
Now that my life force ebbs away,
The world is also coming to an end.

THE PEDDLER-WITCH

Good sirs, go not so quickly by,
Nor miss this opportunity!
Look at my wares attentively,
And many a curious thing you'll spy.
For in my booth is really naught   270
Like anything else on earth: here you find
Each object has at some time brought
Damage to the world and humankind.
No dagger is here, save it set blood a-flowing,
No goblet, save it was death-bestowing!
No jewel save it did seduce
A lovable woman; and no sword I lack
Which has not severed a pledge of truth,
Or stabbed an adversary in the back.

MEPHISTOPHELES

Gossip, you are out of date!   280
What's done is past, what's past is done.
Get in a stock of novelties!
By novelties only are we won.

FAUST

If only I don't go mad in such a place!
This fair keeps up at such a pace!

MEPHISTOPHELES

The pack is crowding to the heights above;
You're being shoved, and think you shove.

FAUST

Who is that?

MEPHISTOPHELES

      Watch her with care!
She's Lilith.   290

FAUST

    Who?

MEPHISTOPHELES

        Adam's first wife! Beware,
Lest you be lured by her bright hair,
Her ornament supreme! For this I know:
Once a youth is captured in that snare,
She does not lightly let him go.

FAUST

That old witch and the young one—sitting there—
Seem to have whirled and hopped about for fair.

MEPHISTOPHELES

Today there is no rest for anyone;
Let's join them; come, a new dance has begun.   300

FAUST (*dancing with a young witch*)

    Once I had a lovely dream,
    In which I saw an apple tree;
    Two splendid apples there did gleam,
    And up I climbed, they tempted me!

THE PRETTY WITCH

    Since the days of Paradise,
    Apples have always tempted you;

So I am overjoyed to know
That they grow in my garden too.

MEPHISTOPHELES (*with an old witch*)

Once I had a vicious dream,
In which I saw a cloven tree;   310
It had a dreadful rent and yet,
Ugly as it was, it suited me.

THE OLD WITCH

A hearty welcome to the Knight
Of the Cloven Hoof—and may
He soon attend the cloven tree,
Unless it frightens him away.

THE PROKTOPHANTASMIST*

Damned mob! How dare you be so indiscreet?
Did we not long ago convince you then,
No spirit stands on ordinary feet?
Yet here you are, dancing like other men!   320

THE PRETTY WITCH (*dancing*)

What is he doing at our ball?

FAUST (*dancing*)

Hm! You'll find him anywhere at all.
He sits in judgment while the others dance;
He talks of every step—if aught is missed,
It's just as if the step did not exist;
He's angriest whenever we advance.
If you spin round and round in circles still,
As he does in his ancient mill,
He then will heartily approve of you,
Especially if you listen to him too.   330

---

* "The backside seer"—a caricature in verse of Goethe's contemporary, Friedrich Nicolai.

THE PROKTOPHANTASMIST

I never heard the like! What! You still here?
We've reasoned you away, so disappear!
By no rules can this devil pack be daunted;
We are so clever, yet Tegel still is haunted.
How long I've labored to sweep out such delusions,
Yet never can be rid of these illusions.

THE PRETTY WITCH

You're boring us to death—do go away!

THE PROKTOPHANTASMIST

Spirits, face to face I want to state,
Spirit-despotism I won't tolerate;
My mind will not submit.   340

(*The dance continues.*)

Today
I see there's nothing I can do;
Each journey gives me something, though;
So ere I take my last, I hope to show
How I defeated the Devil—and poets too.

MEPHISTOPHELES

Down in the nearest puddle he will plump;
That is *his* way of seeking alleviation;
He'll cure himself, with leeches on his rump,
Of spirit and of spirit domination.

(*To* FAUST, *who has left the dance*)

Why did you leave that pretty girl   350
Who, as you were dancing, sweetly sang?

FAUST

Because out of her mouth, as she was singing,
Suddenly a little red mouse sprang.

MEPHISTOPHELES

Don't be squeamish! What's there to that?
Enough to know the mouse was never gray!
In a love-hour who would bother anyway?

FAUST

Next I saw . . .

MEPHISTOPHELES

What?

FAUST

Mephisto, do you see . . . yonder . . .
A child who stands alone, so pale, so sweet?   360
She drags herself quite slowly from the place,
As if—as if she walked with fettered feet.
I must confess I seem to see
A likeness to my little Gretchen's face.

MEPHISTOPHELES

That bodes no good to anyone! Let it be!
It's lifeless, an eidolon, a phantasy.
It is not wise to meet it anywhere;
Man's blood congeals before that frozen stare,
And nearly turns to stone. May one suppose
You have heard about the Medusa head?   370

FAUST

Those are indeed eyes of the dead
No loving hand did close!
That is the breast which Gretchen yielded me,
The tender body loved so passionately!

MEPHISTOPHELES

You gullible fool! It's only a magic play
Which each takes for his love in his own way.

'Here ... Through the lips of Faust
Speaks the whole of Romanticism."
Mario Praz, The Romantic Agony.

188   *Faust: Part 1*   p. 25.

FAUST

What ecstasy! What anguish and despair!
From this dread glance I cannot seem to tear
Myself away! Strange . . . this lovely throat
Is circled by a single narrow thread   380
No wider than a knife-edge . . . and it's red!

MEPHISTOPHELES

Quite right! That I also note.
What's more, she takes her head beneath her arm;
Perseus cut it off, yet did no harm.
Still your old desire for phantasy!
Come up that little hill with me;
It's merry there as in the Prater.*
Unless I have gone off my head,
I really see a little theater.
What's going on?   390

SERVIBILIS

                Soon they'll begin
Another piece, the seventh and the last;
Here they usually give that number; today
A dilettante wrote the play,
And dilettanti form the cast.
Excuse me, sirs, when I now disappear,
And like a dilettante raise the curtain.

MEPHISTOPHELES

Dilettanti, when on the Blocksberg I find you here,
My heart rejoices. It's your sphere for certain.

---

* Famous park in Vienna.

XXII

WALPURGIS NIGHT'S DREAM

or

Oberon's and Titania's Golden Wedding

Intermezzo

THE STAGE MANAGER

Here we shall repose at last,
Mieding's sons* so true;
These old hills and misty vales
For scenery will do.

THE HERALD

To have a golden wedding,
Let fifty years fly by;
Yet it would seem more *golden*
Were quarreling to die.

OBERON

Spirits, if you're really here,
Manifest it now;
For your king and lovely queen
Renew the marriage vow.

10

PUCK

Here is Puck who spins around
And marks time with his feet;

---

* Johann Martin Mieding was the designer and maker of the scenery
at the Weimar court theater of which Goethe was manager. His
"sons" here would be his successors, who can take a rest because
nature supplies the scenery.

Hundreds follow him about,
Sharing in the treat.

ARIEL

Ariel produces song
Clear as a heavenly bell;
Many a fright it can entice,
Pretty ones as well.   20

OBERON

Couples, if you would agree,
Hearken to what we state!
If you wish to stay in love,
Quickly separate!

TITANIA

If he scolds or she be cross,
Seize the pair, be bold!
Take her to a sunny clime,
Take him where the winds blow cold.

ORCHESTRA TUTTI (*fortissimo*)

Snouts of flies, mosquito bills,
Relatives who are patricians,   30
Frogs in moss, crickets in grass,
These are our musicians.

SOLO

Look, here come the bagpipes now!
Soap bubbles, I suppose!
Hear the schnecke-schnicke-schnack,
Through each stumpy nose!

A SPIRIT IN EMBRYO

Belly of toad, the spider's feet,
And little midge's wings

Do not make a little animal,
Yet a little poem sings.   40

A YOUNG COUPLE

Tiny steps and lofty leaps
Through dew and breezy flights;
Although you neatly trip along,
You never reach the heights.

AN INQUISITIVE TRAVELER

Can this be a masquerade?
Can I trust my eyes?
Is Oberon, the lovely god,
Here without disguise?

AN ORTHODOX PERSON

Not a claw and not a tail!
He's really at this revel;   50
Though very like the Grecian gods,
Perhaps he is the Devil!

AN ARTIST FROM THE NORTH

The sketches I am tossing off
Are trifles light as air;
For my Italian journey though,
In due time I prepare.

THE PURIST

Alas, misfortune led me here!
How indecent! Downright *bad!*
Amongst these witches only two
Are in powder clad.   60

A YOUNG WITCH

Powder, like a petticoat,
Suits gray and wrinkled faces;

So I sit naked on my goat
And show my body's graces.

A MATRON

We've really too much *savoir-faire*,
To squabble with you here;
Despite your tender youth, I hope
To see you rot, my dear!

THE LEADER OF THE ORCHESTRA

Snouts of flies, mosquito bills,
Don't crowd around the nude!
Frogs in moss, crickets in grass,
Keep time, and don't be rude!

70

A WEATHER VANE (*on one side*)

Society—the sort one likes!
And brides—why, quite a few!
Bachelors, hm—I do declare!
What a hopeful crew!

A WEATHER VANE (*on the other side*)

If the earth won't open wide
To swallow this rubbish heap,
Then I will give a nimble jump
And into Hell I'll leap!

80

XENIES

With tiny, sharply pointed claws,
As insects we appear;
Satan, our dear papa,
We lovingly revere.

HENNINGS

Look! In crowds quite thickly massed,
All naively jest.
In the end they're sure to say
Their motives were the best.

MUSAGETES

I'd dearly like to lose myself
Amongst this witches' band;   90
Frankly, I find it easier
Than the Muses to command.

A ONE-TIME GENIUS

With the right people, one becomes someone!
Grab my coattails for salvation!
The Blocksberg, like the German Parnassus,
Has quite a broad elevation.

AN INQUISITIVE TRAVELER

Who's that fellow strutting 'round,
With silly airs and graces?
He sniffs at everything he spies.
"He's on a Jesuit's traces!"   100

A CRANE

In clearest brooks I like to fish,
Likewise in muddy streams;
Thus one may see a pious man
Consort with devils, it seems.

A WORLDLING

Yes, everything may serve the ends
Of pious folks, I know;
Upon the Blocksberg they erect
Tabernacles in a row.

A DANCER

Another chorus? I declare,
I hear a distant strumming!   110
"Don't worry! It is in the reeds,
The bitterns' steady drumming."

THE DANCING MASTER

Each one nimbly, stepping high,
Deftly steps they took!
The crooked jumped, the awkward hopped—
What matter how they look!

A JOLLY GOOD FELLOW

The rabble hate each other so,
They'd kill, to say the least;
The bagpipe draws, like Orpheus' lyre,
Every savage beast.   120

A DOGMATIST

I'll not be falsely led astray
By doubts that critics see.
The Devil really must exist;
Else how could devils be?

AN IDEALIST

This phantasy within my mind
Is really much too glowing.
If all I see is really *me*,
Then silly I am growing!

THE REALIST

Living is a dreadful bore,
My grievance is complete;   130
Now for the first time do I feel
Unfirm upon my feet.

THE SUPERNATURALIST

With utmost pleasure I have come,
Well pleased with all I view,
Since from the devils I foretell
The ways of angels too.

THE SCEPTIC

They track the little will-o'-the-wisp,
Treasure they think is near.
As "doubt" is "devil," and "devil" "doubt,"
With pleasure I appear.   140

THE LEADER OF THE ORCHESTRA

Frogs in moss, crickets in grass,
Dilettanti, damned unruly!
Snouts of flies, mosquito bills,
Ye are musicians, truly!

THE ADROIT ONES

Sans souci this troupe is called
Of creatures most entrancing.
As on our feet we can't progress,
On our heads we are advancing.

THE AWKWARD ONES

We sponged on others just a bit,
Now God must help us out!   150
Since we have danced right through our shoes,
Barefoot we skip about.

WILL-O'-THE-WISPS

Out of marshy swamps we come,
Whence first our family sprang;
In sparkling ranks we take our place,
A gallant, glittering gang.

THE SHOOTING STAR

Down from the heights I darted fast,
Trailing sparks and fire;
Now I lie crumpled in the grass,
Who'll help to raise me higher?   160

THE HEAVY ONES

Room! Make room! On every side
The lawn is trodden down;
Here are spirits, spirits who
Have limbs so plump and brown.

PUCK

Don't enter like young elephants,
With such a heavy tramp!
Today the very plumpest one
Is Puck, the hardy scamp.

ARIEL

If loving Nature or the soul
To you a wing discloses,   170
Then follow fast my airy trail
Up the hill of roses!

THE ORCHESTRA (*pianissimo*)

Veils of mist and drifting clouds
Aloft are shining bright.
Breeze in leaves, wind in reeds,
All vanishes from sight!

XXIII

A DISMAL DAY

A field

FAUST   MEPHISTOPHELES

FAUST

In misery! In despair! Despondent and distraught, wandering pitiably for a long time over the face of the earth, and now imprisoned! That lovely, unfortunate creature, under lock and key, a prisoner, abandoned to appalling torment! Has it come to this! to this! . . . Treacherous, contemptible spirit, and you concealed it from me! Stand still—stand still! Roll those devilish eyes wrathfully in your head! Stand still and defy me with your unbearable presence! Imprisoned! Lost in hopeless misery! Delivered over to evil spirits and to the pitiless judgment of men! And meanwhile you lulled me with insipid distraction; you concealed from me her increasing misfortune and allowed her to slide helplessly into ruin!

MEPHISTOPHELES

She is not the first.

FAUST

Dog! Monster of abomination! . . . O thou Infinite Spirit, transform this reptile again into his dog form! Transform him into the shape in which it pleased him so often to caper before me at night, rolling at the feet of a harmless wayfarer, hanging upon his shoulders if he stumbled and fell. Transform him into his favorite likeness, that he may crawl upon his belly before me in the dust, that I may trample him underfoot, the outcast! Not the first! . . . Oh, the sorrow, the pity of it all! It is more than any human soul can grasp! That more than one being should sink into this dark misery, that the first who writhed in this death agony should not have sufficiently expiated the guilt of all others before the eyes of the Eternal Redeemer! The misery of this one soul pierces to the very marrow of my being—yet you grin complacently at the fate of thousands!   30

MEPHISTOPHELES

Now we are again at our wit's end, since we have reached the border line where human senses fail. Why do you seek our companionship if you cannot see it through? You wish to fly, and yet are not immune from dizziness? Come, come! Did we thrust ourselves upon you, or you upon us?

FAUST

Do not bare those voracious teeth at me! It disgusts me! O thou mighty, glorious Spirit, thou who   40 once deignedst to appear before me, thou who dost know my heart and soul, why dost thou chain me to this infamous companion, who feeds upon suffering, who gratifies his thirst upon ruin and desolation?

MEPHISTOPHELES

Have you finished?

FAUST

Rescue her or beware! An appalling curse, a curse of a thousand years be upon you!

MEPHISTOPHELES

I cannot loosen the bonds of the Avenger nor draw the bolts of his locks. Rescue her! Hm—who caused her ruin? I, or you?

(FAUST *gazes wildly about him.*)

So you're reaching for thunderbolts? Fortunately 50 this power has not been vouchsafed to you wretched mortals! It is the way of a tyrant to crush an innocent adversary, to free himself from a dilemma.

FAUST

Take me to her! She shall be free!

MEPHISTOPHELES

What of the danger to which you will be exposed? Remember that bloodguilt—and from your hand—is still upon the town. Avenging spirits hover around the place where the victim fell, lying in wait for the return of the murderer.

FAUST

This too, from you? May a world of death and 60 destruction overwhelm you! Monster! Lead me there, I tell you, and set her free!

MEPHISTOPHELES

I will lead you there: listen to what I *can* do! Am I all-powerful in Heaven and on earth? I will befuddle the senses of the jailer; you get possession of his keys and lead her forth with human hand. I will keep watch! The magic horses are ready! I will carry you both away. This much I can do.

FAUST

Up and away!

XXIV

NIGHT

An open field

Faust *and* Mephistopheles *dash furiously across the field on black horses.*

FAUST

What are they plotting
Yonder round the gallows tree?

MEPHISTOPHELES

I know neither what they are doing
Nor brewing.

FAUST

Soaring and sweeping,
Bending and bowing!

MEPHISTOPHELES

A witch-tribe!

FAUST

Sprinkling and strewing,
A consecrating rite!

MEPHISTOPHELES

Pass on! Pass on!   10

XXV

DUNGEON

Faust *enters with a bunch of keys and a little lamp, and stops before a small iron door.*

FAUST

O'er me a long unwonted shudder falls,
The misery of humankind sweeps over me.
Here she lives, behind these damp, gray walls,
And yet her crime was but a fond delusion!
You draw away, you hesitate,
You fear to see her. . . . On! On!
Death draws nearer while you vacillate!

(*He seizes the keys. The sound of singing is heard within.*)

My mother, the harlot,
She put me to death!
My father, the scoundrel,   10
He fed on my flesh!
My dear little sister
Laid all my bones
In a dark shady place
Under the stones.
Then I changed to a wood-bird,
Fluttering and gay!
Fly away! Fly away! Fly away!

FAUST (*unlocking the door*)

She does not sense her lover is listening,
And hears the rustling straw, the clanking chain.   20

(*He enters.*)

MARGARETE (*hiding herself upon the pallet*)

Dear God! Dear God! They've come!
O bitter death!

FAUST (*softly*)

Hush! Hush! I've come to set you free.

MARGARETE (*throwing herself before him*)

Oh, if you are human, feel for me!

FAUST (*taking hold of the chains to unlock them*)

You will rouse the night guard from his sleep!

MARGARETE (*on her knees*)

Who gave you this authority,
Headsman! over me?
Only midnight, yet you've come for me!
Show mercy to me, let me live!
Will it not be time enough at dawn?   30

(*She rises.*)

And I am still so young, so young!
Yet I must die at morn!
Once I was pretty, *that* was my undoing.
My belovèd was near, now he is far from me.
My wreath is torn, its flowers scattered too.
Do not take hold of me so violently!
Spare me! What have I ever done to you?
Let me not plead in vain, I do implore!
No, I've never seen you in all my life before.

FAUST

How shall I survive this misery!   40

MARGARETE

I am wholly in your might!
But let me nurse my child before I go,
I held it to my heart all night;
They took it from me—to worry me, I know—
And say I killed it. That is what they say!
Never, never shall I be happy more!
They make up songs about me! How wicked to lie!
An old, old tale ends this way.
I wonder who knows why!

FAUST (*falling to his knees*)

One who loves you is at your feet,   50
To free you from the bondage of despair.

MARGARETE (*throwing herself toward him*)

Oh, let us kneel and call upon the saints!
Look! Beneath this very stair
Beneath this threshold
Hell seethes! And it seems
The Evil One,
In terrible wrath,
Rages and screams.

FAUST (*loudly*)

Gretchen! Gretchen!

MARGARETE (*listening attentively*)

That was the voice of my beloved!   60

(*She springs to her feet, and the chains fall off.*)

Where is he? I heard him calling me!
No one shall stop me—I am free!
I'll fly into his arms again,

I'll lie against his heart as well!
He called me Gretchen! . . . And stood there, at the door!
Amidst the howling and clapping sounds of Hell,
Amidst the wrathful, infernal scorn,
I knew the sound of his dear voice once more.

FAUST

'Tis I!

MARGARETE

You! Oh, say it once again!   70

(*She embraces him.*)

'Tis he! 'Tis he! Where now my anguish, my pain?
Where the terror of the dungeon? the chain?
'Tis you! Coming to rescue me!
I'm saved! . . . Ah, once again I see
The street in which I saw you first,
The garden bright with flowers too,
Where Marthe and I awaited you.

FAUST (*pleadingly*)

Come with me! Come!

MARGARETE

Oh, stay with me!
Wherever you are, there I love to be!   80

(*She caresses him.*)

FAUST

Hurry! Away!
For unless you hurry,
We shall be made to pay.

MARGARETE

Can you no longer kiss? How's this?
Away from me a little while, my dear,
Yet you've forgotten how to kiss?
Why do I feel so frightened here
In your arms enfolded, when
Once at just a word, a glance,
Heaven itself descended! *Then*   90
You kissed as though you'd stifle me.
Kiss me!
Else I will kiss you—see!

(*She embraces him.*)

Oh, pity me! Your lips are chill
And still!
Where is your love
Hiding?
Who has done me this cruel wrong?

(*She turns away from him.*)

FAUST

Come! Follow me! Sweetheart, be strong!
A thousand times more lovingly I'll kiss,   100
Follow me now! I ask of you only this!

MARGARETE (*coming nearer*)

And is it you? Really, really you?

FAUST

'Tis I! Come with me, come!

MARGARETE

You loose my chain,
You take me on your lap again!

How is it that you do not shrink from me?
Do you know, love, whom you are setting free?

FAUST

Come! Come! Darkness already yields to day.

MARGARETE

I killed my mother,
I drowned my child.
Was it not given to you and to me?   110
To you, too! . . . It's you! . . . I scarce believe it!
Your dear hand! Oh, it's damp! How can that be?
Wipe it off! It would seem
Blood were upon it.
O God! What have you done!
Put that sword away,
I beg of you!

FAUST

Oh, let the past be past!
You'll kill me unless you do.   120

MARGARETE

No, no, belovèd, you must survive!
I will describe to you with care
The graves tomorrow to prepare:
The best place you must give to mother,
And close beside her lay my brother.
To one side, somewhere, let me stay,
Only not too far away!
And the child at my right breast,
No one else will ever lie near!
Oh, what sweet, what holy joy   130
It was to creep beside you, dear!
That will never come to me again.

I feel I must compel myself toward you,
As if you pushed me back with might and main.
Yet it's really you . . . and you seem kind and true.

FAUST

If you feel it's really I, then come!

MARGARETE

Out there?

FAUST

Into freedom.

MARGARETE

If the grave you'll prepare,
If death's lurking there, 140
Then come! From here to eternal rest—
Otherwise, not a step with you!
You're leaving? O love, could I go too!

FAUST

Will it, and you can! The door is wide.

MARGARETE

There is no hope, I dare not step outside.
What use to fly? They'd only hound me out,
Just as before!
Oh, what misery to beg and roam about,
With an evil conscience furthermore!
What misery to wander on each day! 150
And they would catch me anyway!

FAUST

I'll stay with you.

MARGARETE

Quickly! Quickly!
Save your poor child!
Be off! . . . Keep following the path
Up to the brook,
Across . . . across where the old bridge stood,
Deep in the wood!
Left, where the plank lies
In the pool.   160
Seize it, be quick!
It's trying to rise,
Save it! Save it! . . . Oh, see,
How it's wriggling still!

FAUST

Come to yourself!
One step, dear, then you are free!

MARGARETE

If only we were past that hill!
My mother sits there, on top of a stone,
Down me creeps a shiver of dread!
My mother sits there, on top of a stone,   170
To and fro wagging her head;
She can't beckon or nod, her head's heavy and sore,
She slept so long, she will never wake more.
She slept so that we could have joy always!
Oh, those were such happy days!

FAUST

Here words, here prayers are no avail! I see
I must attempt to carry you away.

MARGARETE

Do not grip me so murderously!
Let me go! I will endure no force, I say!
Once I did all for love of you.   180

FAUST

The day is dawning! Love—dear love!

MARGARETE

Dawn? Yes, it is the dawn! The last day hurries on its way;
Why, this should have been my wedding day!
Tell no one you have been with Gretchen—
Alas, my wreath! . . .
All's over now! . . . Once more plain,
We shall see each other again,
But it will not be at a dance.
The crowd is gathering, silent as in a trance.
The streets, the square,   190
Scarce hold them there.
The death bell tolls, the rod is broken.
How they seize me, how they bind me tight!
Now I'm shoved to the block, the knife quivers in fright.
Over everyone's neck as it quivers o'er mine.
And the world lies still as the grave!

FAUST

Oh, had I never been born!

(MEPHISTOPHELES *appears outside.*)

MEPHISTOPHELES

Away! Else both are lost! Away!
Useless chatter! Talk, talk, and delay!
My horses are neighing and shaking,   200
Dawn is breaking.

MARGARETE

What's rising up before me? His face!
Send him away! *'Tis he! 'Tis he!*
What does he want here, in this holy place?
Ah . . . he wants *me!*

FAUST

You shall live!

MARGARETE

Judgment of God! I give myself to Thee!

MEPHISTOPHELES

Come! Or I'll desert you both immediately.

MARGARETE

Save me! Father, I am thine!
Ye Angels! Ye Celestials too, appear!
Range yourselves to guard me here!
Love, I am aghast at what you are!

MEPHISTOPHELES

She is doomed!

VOICE FROM ABOVE

Is saved!

MEPHISTOPHELES (*to* FAUST)

Hither to me!

(*He disappears with* FAUST.)

A VOICE (*from within, dying away*)

Belovèd . . . Belovèd!